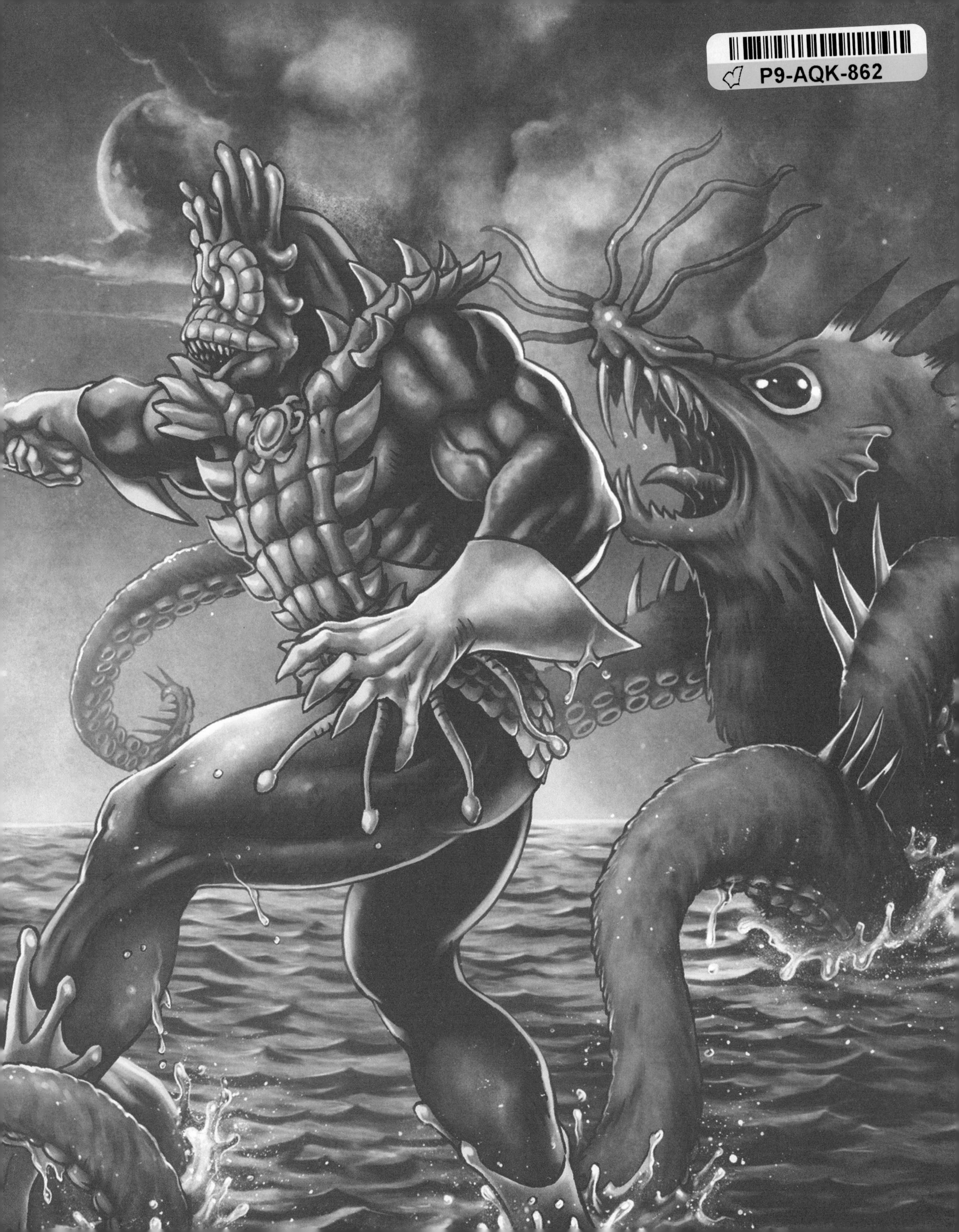

THE MASTERS OF THE UNIVERSE BOOK

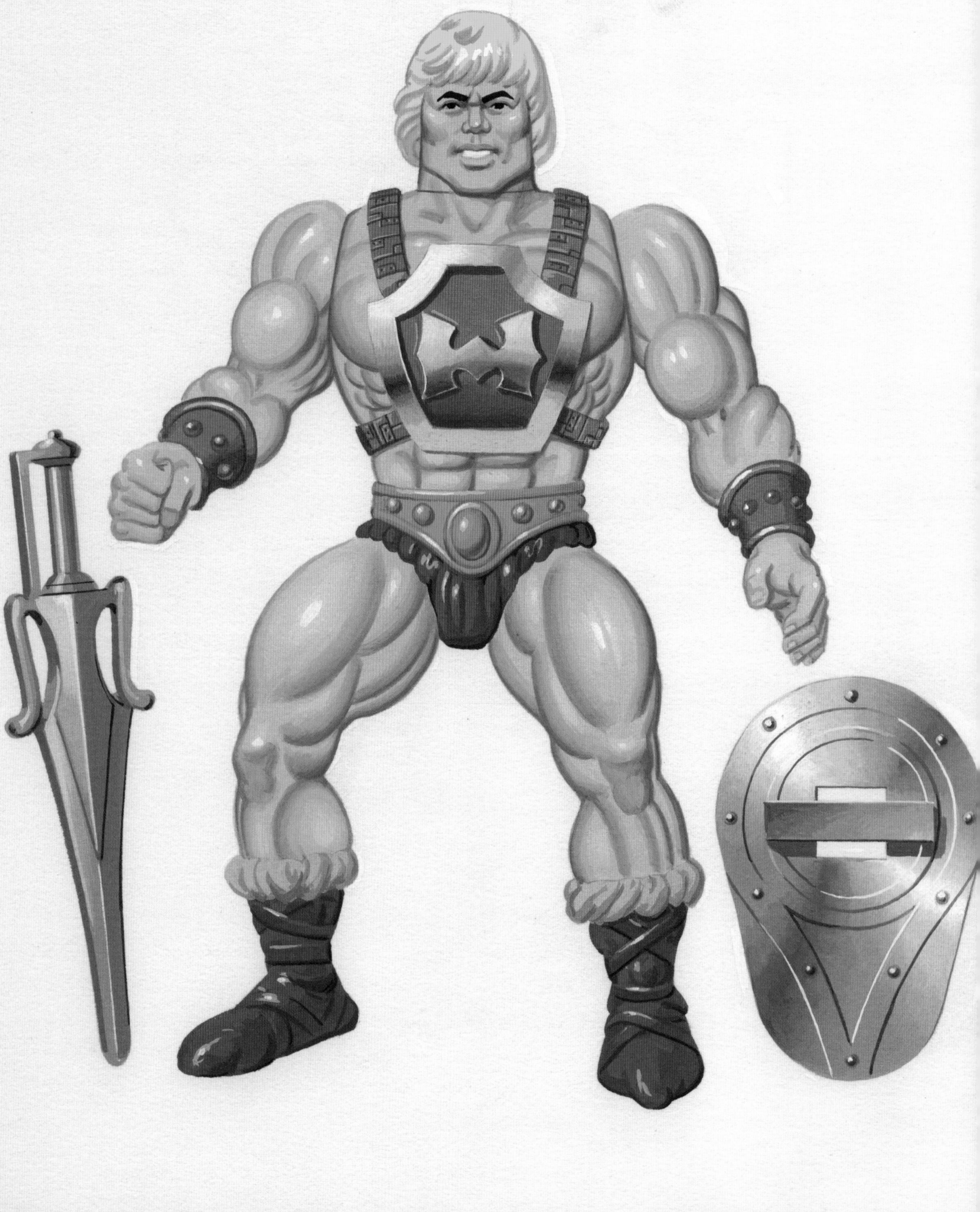

THE

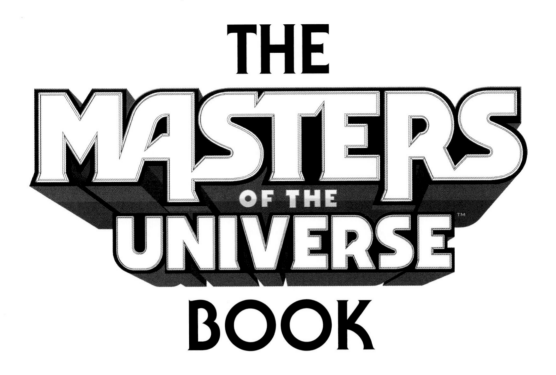

MASTERS
OF THE
UNIVERSE™

BOOK

THE EPIC HISTORY OF HE-MAN, SHE-RA, AND THE MASTERS OF THE UNIVERSE

Written by Simon Beecroft

Contents

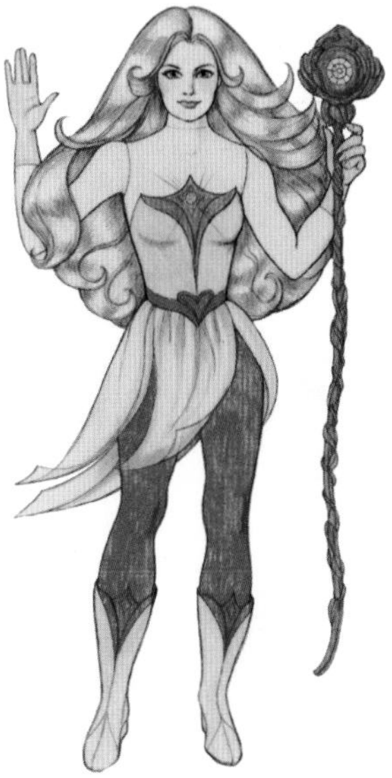

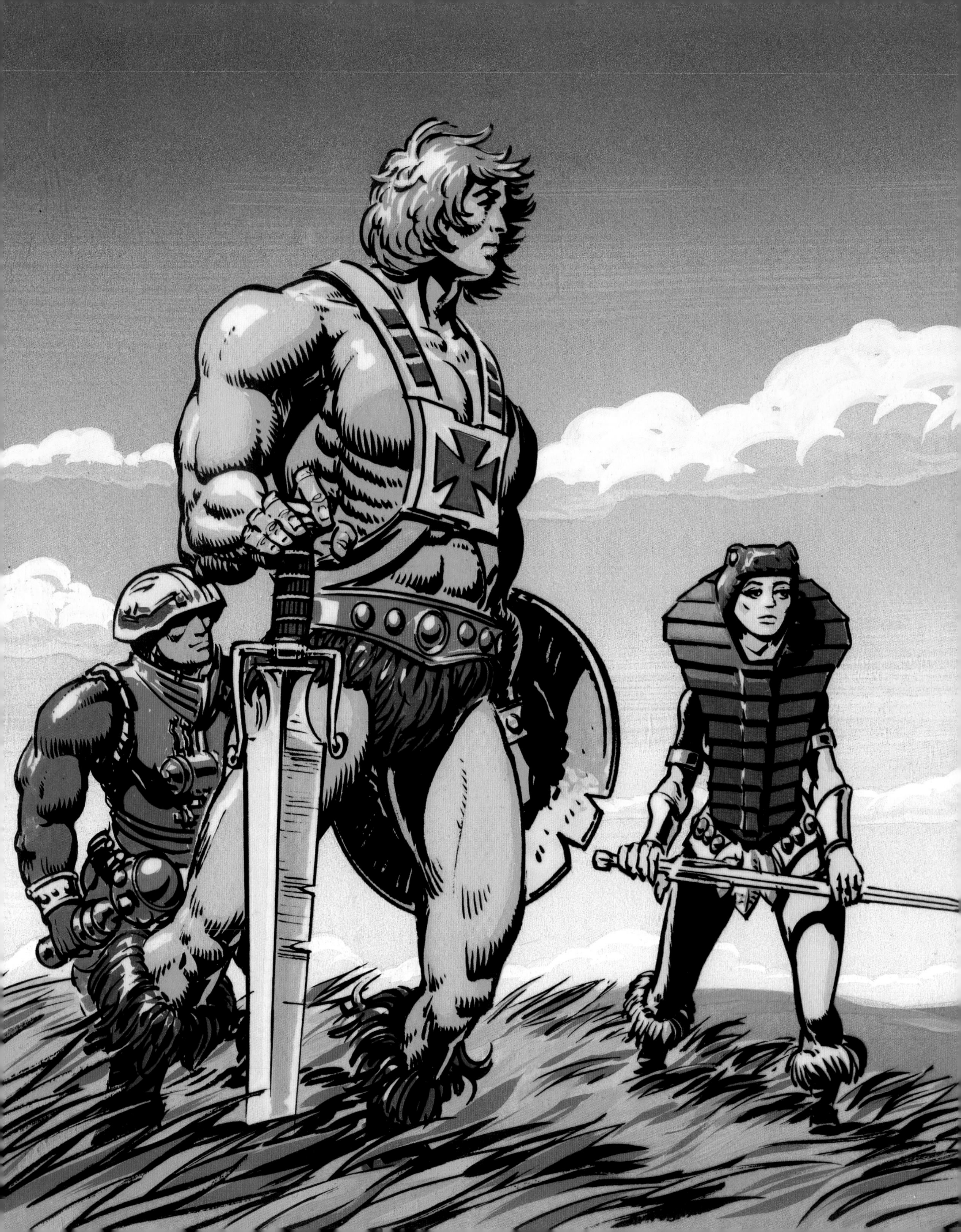

Introduction

Skeletor's skull face, She-Ra's winged crown, the ominous Castle Grayskull, Prince Adam raising his sword and declaring "By the power of Grayskull ..."

The world of He-Man and She-Ra is not short of iconic images. Created in-house at Mattel in the early 1980s, the Masters of the Universe broke the mold in a toy landscape dominated by tie-ins to movie blockbusters. These new heroes existed in a world created initially solely on the page—in comic books—and, only later, in an animated TV show. Mattel's toy team had taken the time to observe how 5-year-olds play with toys, seeing the attraction that young kids have to superhuman strength and power. The toy makers doubled down, giving kids the biggest, most powerful toy character ever made—and they gave him the most outrageously simple name: *He-Man*.

Sure, He-Man is unfeasibly powerful and muscled. But he's also intelligent, articulate, and compassionate; he thinks though problems rather than just bashing through walls; his best friend, Teela, is an equal; and his alter ego, Adam, is all-too-human. Throw in a dad—the king—who doesn't understand him (and a mother who intuitively does); a surrogate father figure in Man-At-Arms; a long-lost sister, Adora, who is secretly a Princess of Power; and an uncle, Keldor, who turns out to become his worst enemy—Skeletor!

The original inspiration may have been sword-and-sorcery fantasy, but in the hands of skilled artists and writers, He-Man became a full-blown soap opera … with swords. And sorcery!

The classic story continues to be retold and reimagined today, with a devoted fan base of all ages, including those who grew up with He-Man and She-Ra in the 1980s—now the adult attendees of fan conventions like Power-Con, held each year in California—as well as a new generation of kids who are discovering the world of excitement and adventure for the very first time.

The following pages bring together many of the highlights of this fascinating, ever-expanding universe, from toys and comics to animation, books, posters, packaging, and movies—with a wealth of fabulous, behind-the-scenes concept art selected from Mattel's archives.

In the 2021 animated series *Masters of the Universe: Revelation*, Skeletor shrieks triumphantly to He-Man, "Let this be our final battle!"

But you know it won't be, not by a long shot. Long may He-Man continue to hold aloft his sword and proclaim:

"I have the power!"

By Simon Beecroft

1980s

Debuting in 1982 with the most muscle-bound action figures ever, He-Man and the Masters of the Universe became a 1980s phenomenon, with its animated TV series and a world of comics, books, games, and much more. She-Ra's debut in 1985 extended the formula for success to action-seeking young girls—many of whom were already Masters fans.

1982
→ Debut of "Masters of the Universe" toy line with minicomics
→ Castle Grayskull play set–like most of the original toys, it was released internationally; for example, as Le Chateau des Ombres in French-speaking countries and Castillo Grayskull in Spanish-speaking countries.
→ First comic books from DC Comics

1983
→ Second year of "Masters of the Universe" toy line
→ DC Comics develops the minicomics packaged with the toys
→ Debut of *He-Man and the Masters of the Universe* Filmation animated series
→ First children's books from Golden Books and Ladybird

1984
→ Third year of "Masters of the Universe" toy line
→ Snake Mountain play set

1985
→ Fourth year of "Masters of the Universe" toy line
→ Second and final series of *He-Man and the Masters of the Universe* animated series
→ Theatrical release of *He-Man and She-Ra: The Secret of the Sword*
→ Debut of *She-Ra: Princess of Power* animated series
→ Debut of "She-Ra Princess of Power" toy line, with minicomics
→ Launch of US-based fan-club magazine *He-Man and the Masters of the Universe*
→ *He-Man and She-Ra: Christmas Special*

1986
→ Fifth year of "Masters of the Universe" toy line
→ Second year of "She-Ra Princess of Power" toy line
→ First comic books from Marvel Comics
→ Debut of "Masters of the Universe" daily syndicated newspaper comic strip
→ Launch of US-based fan-club magazine *She-Ra and the Princesses of Power*
→ Launch of *By The Power Of Grayskull … Masters Of The Universe* comic magazine in the UK

1987
→ Masters of the Universe "Power Tour" live stage show, which toured across the US and Canada
→ Sixth year of "Masters of the Universe" toy line
→ "The Powers of Grayskull" toys
→ Third and final year of "She-Ra Princess of Power" toy line
→ Final episode of *She-Ra: Princess of Power*
→ Theatrical release of live-action *Masters of the Universe: the Motion Picture*

1988
→ Final year of "Masters of the Universe" toy line, released only in Europe

1989
→ Debut of "He-Man" toy line

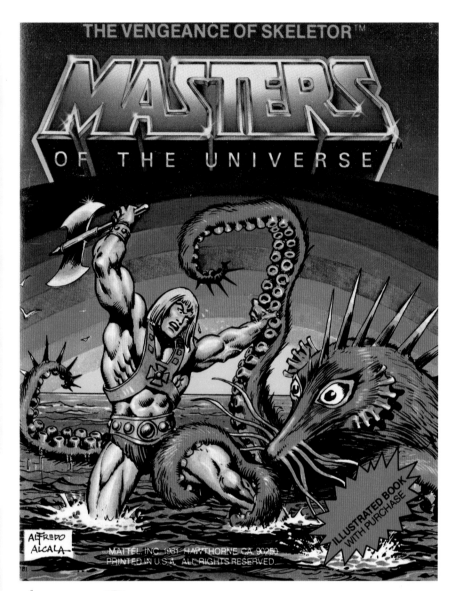

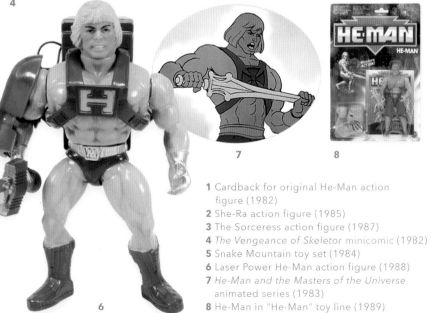

1 Cardback for original He-Man action figure (1982)

2 She-Ra action figure (1985)

3 The Sorceress action figure (1987)

4 *The Vengeance of Skeletor* minicomic (1982)

5 Snake Mountain toy set (1984)

6 Laser Power He-Man action figure (1988)

7 *He-Man and the Masters of the Universe* animated series (1983)

8 He-Man in "He-Man" toy line (1989)

1990s-2000s

He-Man is reinvented as a space explorer in the *The New Adventures of He-Man* animated series, with its accompanying comics and "He-Man" toy line. Then, he laid down his glowing Sword of Power and put up his space boots to sit out the rest of the 1990s. It was in this intervening time that fans began to document and celebrate the history of the toys and the TV show on the then-new Internet. Fully recharged, He-Man burst back into action in the 2000s with toys of hitherto-unseen realism, as well as a new animated series and comic books.

1990
→ Debut of *The New Adventures of He-Man* animated series
→ Second year of "He-Man" toy line

1991
→ Third year of "He-Man" toy line

1992
→ Fourth and final year of "He-Man" toy line

1995
→ First fan sites appear on the Internet, including Keven Hebert's He-Man Page, Jaye's She-Ra Page, and Adam Tyner's He-Man Page

1996
→ Guardians of Grayskull mailing list
→ Scrolls of Grayskull email newsletter

1997
→ He-Man and She-Ra Episode Review website

1999
→ Launch of He-Man.org

2000
→ First year of "Commemorative Series" toy line

2001
→ Second and final year of "Commemorative Series" toy line

2002
→ "Masters of the Universe" toy line sculpted by Four Horsemen Studios
→ Launch of *Masters of the Universe* animated series
→ Tie-in comic books from Image Comics and MVCreations
→ Release of mini-statue figures from NECA

2003
→ Second year of "Masters of the Universe" toy line

9   10   11   12   13   14

1 Nordor play set in "He-Man" toy line (1990)
2 Battle Bird toy in "He-Man" toy line (1991)
3 Battle Blade Skeletor in "He-Man" toy line (1992)
4 "Four Horsemen" She-Ra (2004)

5 "Four Horsemen" TrapJaw (2003)
6 MOTU Classics He-Man (2008)
7 Commemorative Series packaging art (2001)
8 Retailer-exclusive comic book cover (2002)
9 Commemorative Series Mer-Man (2000)

10 Snout Spout "staction figure" (2005)
11 Mantenna "staction figure" (2006)
12 Evil-Lyn "staction figure" (2007)
13 MOTU Classic He-Ro (2009)
14 He-Man.org website (1998)

2004
→ Third and final year of "Masters of the Universe" toy line
→ Final episodes of *Masters of the Universe* animated series
→ Statues sculpted by Four Horsemen Studios for NECA Toys

2005
→ First year of action-figure-size mini-statues ("staction figures")
→ Mini-statues and busts sculpted by Four Horsemen Studios for NECA Toys
→ Debut of DVD series from BCI Eclipse

2006
→ Second year of "staction figures"

2007
→ Third year of "staction figures"

2008
→ Debut of "Masters of the Universe Classics" toy line

2009
→ Second year of "Masters of the Universe Classics" toy line

2010-present

Launched in 2008, the Masters of the Universe Classics toy line has become the largest and longest-running in Masters history. Recent decades have seen nonstop activity for He-Man and She-Ra, with various toy lines aimed at young fans and adult collectors alike. Exclusives are regularly launched at San Diego Comic-Con and the dedicated MOTU convention, Power-Con, run by Val Staples and his army of fan volunteers. With epic comic book sagas like *He-Man: the Eternity War*, and two new animated series debuting on Netflix in 2021, the future for He-Man—and all of Eternia!—is assured.

1

2010
→ Third year of "Masters of the Universe Classics" toy line

2011
→ First Power-Con held in Los Angeles, CA
→ Fourth year of "Masters of the Universe Classics" toy line

2012
→ *Masters of the Universe* eight-issue digital comic-book series from DC Comics
→ *He-Man and the Masters of the Universe* six-issue comic-book series from DC Comics
→ *He-Man and the Masters of the Universe Origins* comic-book series from DC Comics
→ Minicomics for "Masters of the Universe Classics" toy line from Dark Horse
→ Fifth year of "Masters of the Universe Classics" toy line
→ *He-Man: the Most Powerful Game in the Universe* app game and *She-Ra: the Most Powerful Update in the Universe*

2013
→ *He-Man and the Masters of the Universe* ongoing comic-book series from DC Comics
→ *DC Universe vs. Masters of the Universe* crossover comic-book series from DC Comics
→ Sixth year of "Masters of the Universe Classics" toy line

2014
→ Debut of "Masters of the Universe Minis" toy line in two-packs
→ Debut of "Masters of the Universe Giants" toy line
→ Seventh year of "Masters of the Universe Classics" toy line
→ "He-Man: The Eternity War" 15-issue comic-book series from DC Comics

2015
→ Second year of "Masters of the Universe Giants" toy line
→ *The Art of He-Man and the Masters of the Universe* from Dark Horse
→ *He-Man and the Masters of the Universe: Minicomic Collection* from Dark Horse
→ Eighth year of "Masters of the Universe Classics" toy line

2016
→ Debut of "Masters of the Universe" toy line from Super7
→ Debut of Club Grayskull "He-man and the Masters of the Universe" toy line, based on the Filmation animated series
→ "He-Man/ThunderCats" six-issue crossover comic-book series from DC Comics
→ "Masters of the Universe Classics" toy line now from Super7
→ *He-Man and She-Ra: A Complete Guide to the Classic Animated Adventures* from Dark Horse
→ *He-Man: Tappers of Grayskull* gaming app

2017
→ *The Toys that Made Us: He-Man* documentary

→ *He-Man and the Masters of the Universe: A Character Guide and World* Companion from Dark Horse

→ *He-Man and the Masters of the Universe: The Newspaper Comic Strips* from Dark Horse

2018

→ *She-Ra and the Princesses of Power* animated series from Netflix and DreamWorks

→ *Injustice vs. Masters of the Universe* six-part crossover comic-book series from DC Comics

→ *Power of Grayskull: The Definitive History of He-Man and the Masters of the Universe* documentary airs on Netflix

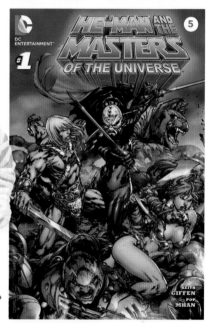

2019

→ "Masters of the Universe Origins" toy line launched at San Diego Comic-Con

→ Debut of "She-Ra and the Princesses of Power" toy line based on Netflix/Dreamworks animated series

→ Launch of *He-Man and the Masters of the Multiverse* six-issue limited comic-book series from DC Comics

2020

→ First full year of "Masters of the Universe Origins" toy line

→ "Masters of the Universe Minis" figures in single-packs

2021

→ *Masters of the Universe: Revelation* on Netflix

→ *He-Man and the Masters of the Universe* CGI series on Netflix

→ *Masters of the Universe:* Masterverse toy line

→ *He-Man and the Masters of the Universe* toy line for CGI series

→ Debut of *Masters of the Universe: Revelation* prequel comic-book series from Dark Horse

→ Second year of "Masters of the Universe Origins" toy line

→ *The Toys of He-Man and the Masters of the Universe* from Dark Horse

2022

→ Third year of "Masters of the Universe Origins" toy line

1 MOTU Classics She-Ra (2010)
2 MOTU Classics Glimmer (2014)
3 Cosplay at Power-Con
4 *Masters of the Universe: The Lost Knight* digital comic (2012)
5 *He-Man and the Masters of the Universe* Issue #1 (2013)
6 Super7 Possessed Skeletor (2016)
7 *The Newspaper Comic Strips* from Dark Horse (2017)
8 *He-Man and the Masters of the Multiverse* Issue #1 (2020)

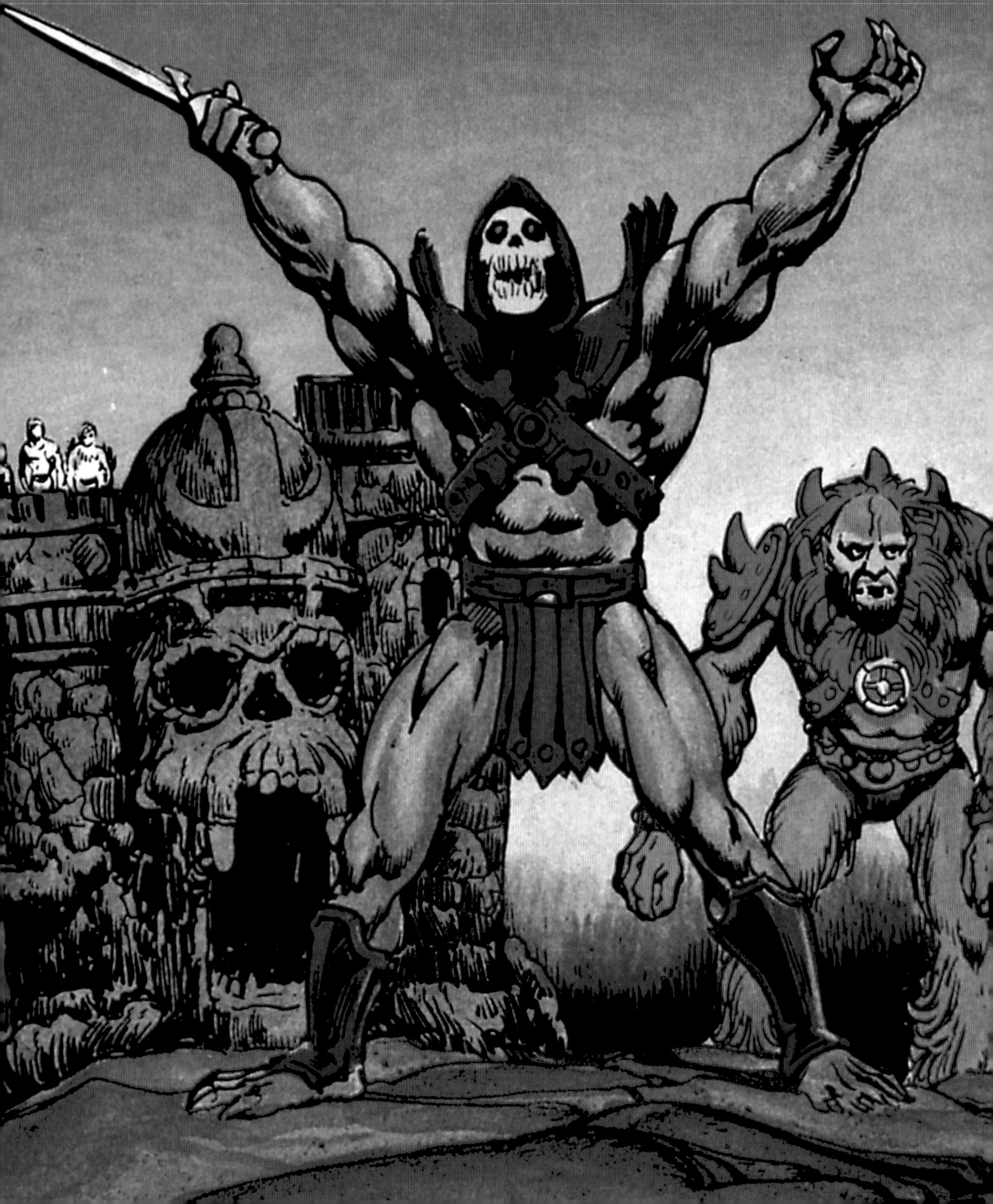

ORIGINS

"Legend tells of a warrior who will find the split halves of the Power Sword ..."

Spirit of Castle Grayskull, "King of Castle Grayskull," 1981

Skeletor, Beast Man, and Mer-Man from "The Vengeance of Skeletor" minicomic *(left)* and He-Man action figure *(right)*

A New Hero

After Mattel declined an offer in 1976 to produce toys for the then-unreleased *Star Wars*, the commercial success of George Lucas's film and its merchandise prompted the toy company to seek its own boys' action line.

From its then-home in Hawthorne, California, Mattel dominated the market for toy dolls and toy cars with Barbie and Hot Wheels, and now the company was seeking similar success with boys' action figures. Its biggest success so far had been Big Jim, an all-purpose action-sports-spy hero launched in the early 1970s. After the explosion of *Star Wars* toys from Kenner, Mattel had bought in licenses based on movies and TV, including *Battlestar Galactica*, *Flash Gordon*, and *Clash of the Titans*. Then, a new idea emerged: to create an original property that would be its own, not bought-in. Mattel asked its team of in-house designers to come up with a new theme that could compete with *Star Wars* (no pressure!). Various concepts were tried—giants and goblins among them—but none received an overwhelmingly positive reaction at the company's product conferences. Mattel's marketing team decided to undertake some primary research: They watched how 5-year-old boys played with toys. They could see that boys were drawn to "strength, fierceness, and superhuman powers." The children acted out being in control and having great power. Inspiration struck: The team decided to create the biggest, most powerful action character ever.

August 15, 1979

TO: Distribution
FROM: Ray Wagner
SUBJECT: Category Management Teams

You have been selected as a member of a Category Team. You are about to have a very important role in the development of the 3-Year Business Plan for that category.

To introduce you to the subject of Category Management, our goals and objectives, and how to prepare a Business Plan, I have scheduled an all-day session Thursday, August 23 at the Hacienda Hotel. Your attendance at this session is requested.

Thank you.

RW/pr

Hacienda Hotel
525 No. Sepulveda Blvd.
El Segundo, CA

↑ Mattel CEO Ray Wagner sent an internal memo to relevant parties within the company inviting them to a meeting at the Hacienda Hotel in El Segundo, California, near their office, to explore ideas for an action figure line.

↑ Mark Taylor's early concept art established many of He-Man's attributes, including his chest harness, belt, loin cloth, gauntlets, and helmet. He-Man's Sword of Power arrived later in the process—for now, he was an ax-wielder.

→ Mark Taylor worked on more detailed conceptualization of the action figure, still with a prominent ax and horned helmet, and a knife tucked into his boot.

GENESIS OF HE-MAN

Mattel artist Mark Taylor was brought in, chosen for the closeness of his style to legendary fantasy artist Frank Frazetta, a key inspiration for the new concept. A fan of Harold R. Foster's classic Arthurian comic strip *Prince Valiant* and EC Comics' horror and suspense titles such as *Weird Tales,* Taylor had already invented his own fantasy character, who he called "Torak—Hero of Prehistory." This barbarian eventually morphed into a powerful new ax-wielding, loin-cloth-wearing titan. With the first three-dimensional prototypes created by another Mattel artist, Roger Sweet, He-Man was born!

"The Good Guy is always the favorite; he is powerful and he is inevitably triumphant in the end."

Early production notes, 1981

← Mark Taylor created an illustration of a long-haired character dressed in animal furs called "Vikor." For many iterations, the character who would become He-Man would wear a horned helmet and carry a battle ax.

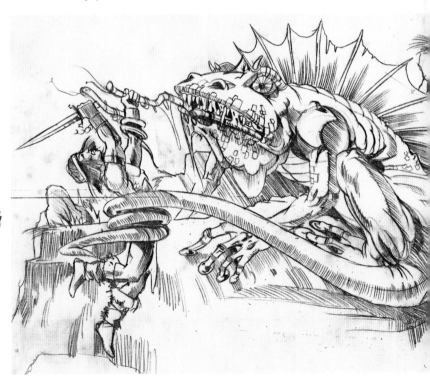

↑ He-Man, now grasping a sword, is dark haired in this art by Mark Taylor. He became blond to more closely resemble Tom Kalinske, who was then in Mattel's upper management!

He-Man Prototypes

In 1980, Mattel designer Roger Sweet made three prototype action figures of a new hero. He took Big Jim figures from an existing Mattel toy line and bulked them up with modeling clay to create eye-popping muscular physiques the likes of which had never been seen before in a boys' toy. One of them, a military-themed figure, wore a tank turret on his head and was called Tank Head. Another wore a sci-fi-inspired helmet and was called Bullet Head. The third figure was a fantasy barbarian with a bearskin cape and a battle ax, named He-Man. Sweet very deliberately posed his characters in battle-ready stances, making them instantly more engaging than existing boys' action figures, which tended to have stiff, upright positions. For additional impact, he gave his barbarian a bared-teeth expression. At 9½ inches (24 cm) tall, Sweet's figures were designed to impress—the actual figures in the line from 1982–1988 would be smaller, at 5½ inches (14 cm)—and in this he was successful. When Mattel CEO Ray Wagner saw them, his instant reaction was, "These have the power!"

> "Let's do something that's just massive and makes every other action figure look wimpy."
>
> Roger Sweet, former Mattel designer, 2017

FIRST PROTOTYPE
In one of the trio of figures hand-sculpted by Roger Sweet, He-Man wears a recognizable version of the battle harness, designed by Mark Taylor.

CLAY MODEL
This 1981 clay model by Mattel artist Tony Guerrero is closer to the final He-Man design, with his loin cloth and belt.

HEROIC FIGURE
Many more prototypes were sculpted as He-Man was developed. In this hand-colored version by Tony Guerrero, the hero still wears the horned helmet often seen in many of the first conceptualizations by Mark Taylor.

Creating Skeletor

The very embodiment of bone-chilling evil, Skeletor's origins lie in a childhood trip to a macabre exhibit in an amusement park.

↑ Before Skeletor, Mark Taylor created a green-skinned monstrosity known as Demo-Man, short for "Demon-Man," as an evil counterpart to He-Man.

Mattel artist Mark Taylor created the first images of the character who would become the cackling, skeleton-faced ghoul we all love to hate. "Skeletor became the very essence of evil," he said. "He actually represents fear." When the artist was a child, his parents took him to the Pike, an amusement zone in Long Beach, California. In the House of Fear, Taylor encountered an exhibit that haunted him into adulthood: what looked like the dead body of a man suspended from the ceiling. To young, terrified Mark, it smelled and looked like a real dead body. In truth, it was: American outlaw Elmer McCurdy was killed in a shoot-out with police and his mummified body was displayed to the public from the 1920s to the 1960s. "That was one of the scariest things I've ever seen," said Taylor. "And that's where Skeletor came from." A keen fan of fantasy art and literature from childhood, Taylor had sketched a character, Torak–Hero of Prehistory, who became a significant part of the inspiration for He-Man. But if you look at the background of this very early drawing, Taylor had sketched in a menacing figure: inspired visually by the fairground exhibit, but also his own interest in literature and in the iconography of the Mexican Day of the Dead, this would become Skeletor. "If you have a good guy," noted Taylor, "you measure the good guy by the bad guy."

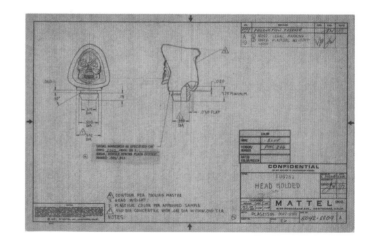

↑ A technical drawing of Skeletor's head shows the precise measurements and other information needed for the action-figure mold.

'D MAN.

Mark Taylor drew this early
version of Skeletor's action
figure. The ram's skull at the
top of the Havoc Staff was
intended to pop off and was
attached to the staff by string.

K06827

HEAD
LT ARM
RT ARM   PMS
TORSO U/R   550
"   U/F
"   L/R
"   L/F
LEG   RT
"   LT.

MOULD.
HEAD TO
GET HOOD
COLOR — PMS
266

LOWER
TORSO

| PANTONE | PANTONE |
| 550C | 266 |

5042

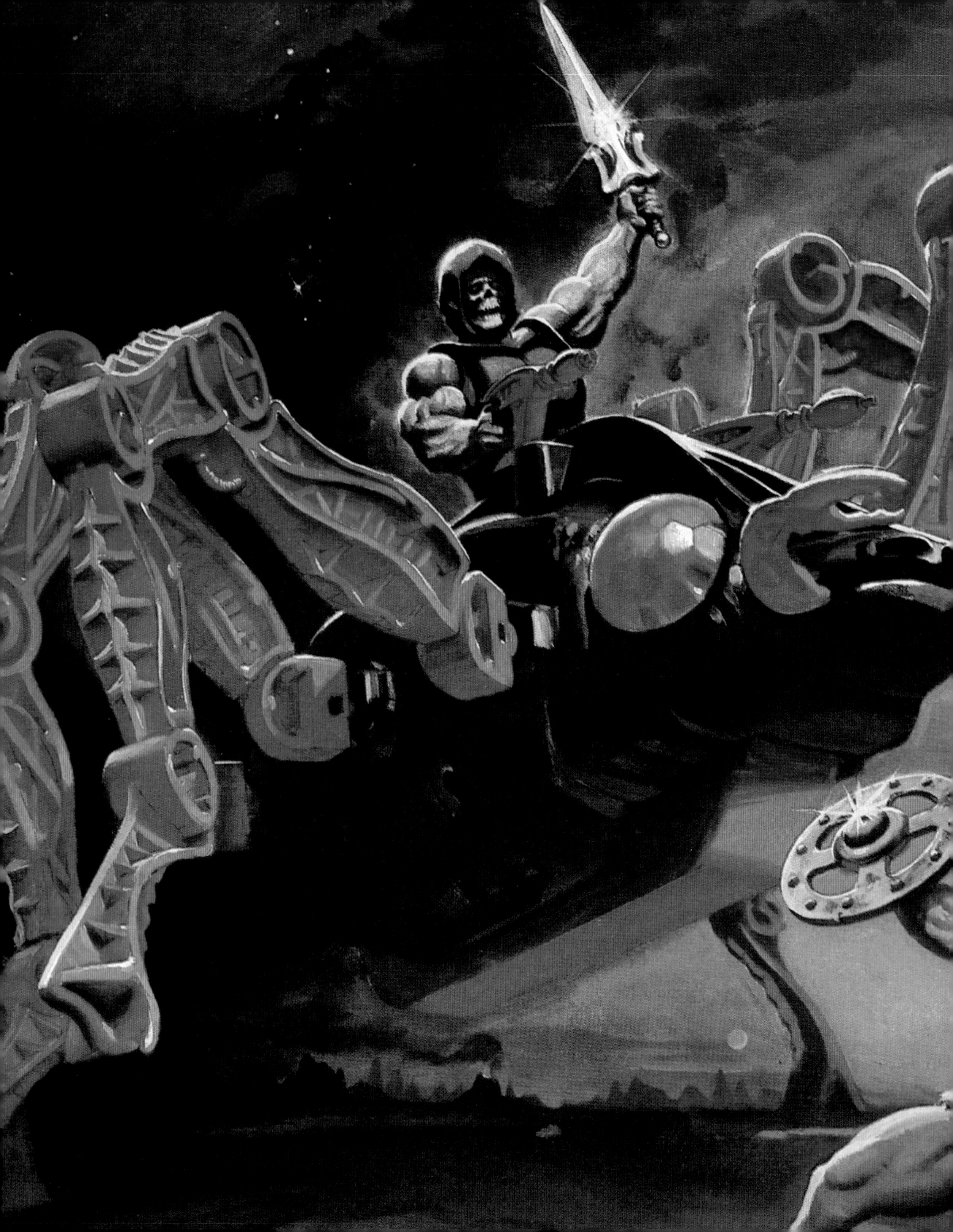

S words and sorcery co-exist with futuristic
technology in the world of He-Man and the
Masters of the Universe. This striking fusion
is captured perfectly in illustrations that artists such
as William George and Rudy Obrero created for
toy packaging (George's Spydor, *left*) and Fred
Carillo and others created for the earliest books
in 1982 (Battle Ram, *above*). Befitting its original
inspiration in the fantasy and science-fiction art of
Frank Frazetta, much of the art created for the line
in the 1980s was painterly, powerfully atmospheric,
often surprisingly dark, and always thrilling.

The Heroic Warriors

Masters of the Universe action figures hit stores in 1982 at an impressive 5½ inches (14 cm) tall—nearly 2 inches (5 cm) taller than Kenner's *Star Wars* and Hasbro's *G.I. Joe: A Real American Hero* lines. The first wave established the core characters of He-Man and his heroic allies— Man-At-Arms, Teela, Stratos, Zodac, and Battle Cat—facing off against Skeletor and the Evil Warriors. Over the next five years, each wave of toys offered new characters and novelty features. Man-E-Faces, released in 1983, had a dial on his head to turn his face from human to robot to monster, while Mekaneck in 1984 had an extendible neck. In 1985, Moss Man was covered in green flocking and "real pine scent." Innovations for 1986 included Snout Spout, who squirted water out of his nose-trunk, and transforming Meteorbs such as Tuskor. Finally, 1987 saw the appearance of Bionatops, a bionic dinosaur, one of the few toys released in a proposed (but canceled) spin-off line, "The Powers of Grayskull."

One half of the Power Sword (Skeletor has the other half)

Battle ax

Spring-back mechanism in waist delivers "power punch"

HE-MAN

Removable armored saddle and helmet

Clip-on wings

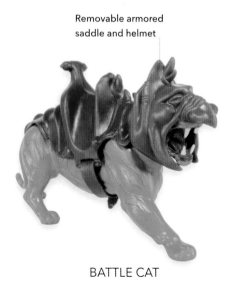

BATTLE CAT

MAN-AT-ARMS

TEELA

STRATOS

SNOUT SPOUT

MOSS MAN

MAN-E-FACES

MEKANECK

RIO BLAST

ROKKON

EXTENDAR

Extends by
2 1/2 inches
(6.3 cm)

CLAMP CHAMP

PRINCE ADAM

BATTLE ARMOR
HE-MAN

ROTAR

Spins like
a top

Giant figure
stands 15 in
(38 cm) tall!

TYTUS

BIONATOPS

STRIDOR

Tuskor in orb form

TUSKOR

The Warriors of Evil

The first villains to emerge in 1982 were Skeletor and his main henchmen, Mer-Man and Beast Man, followed in 1983 by Evil-Lyn, Faker, Trap Jaw, Tri-Klops, and Skeletor's mount, Panthor. Further waves featured an array of colorful evil-doers. In 1984, the creepy crop included Clawful, with his spring-action pinching claw; Kobra Khan—the Evil Master of Snakes—who squirts a "hypnotic" mist of water; and Webstor, with a working grapple hook. Heinous highlights from 1985 included fur-ball Grizzlor; Mantenna with his pop-out eyes; Stinkor with a powerful repelling scent (of real patchouli oil!); Hordak, the leader of the Evil Horde; and Modulok, with enough parts to transform into a multitude of oddball creatures. In 1986, the Snake Men slithered onto shelves, among them leader King Hiss with a freaky snake body hidden beneath his disguise armor and Sssqueeze, whose long rubber arms with inner wire could be moved into different strangulating positions. The final year, 1987, saw Tyrantisaurus Rex, a bionic Preternian dinosaur in the proposed "The Powers of Grayskull line"— before the toy line itself became extinct.

Purple Sword of Power

Detailed face decoration

Havoc Staff

SKELETOR

Glow-in-the-dark wand

MER-MAN

BEAST MAN

EVIL-LYN

TRI-KLOPS

PANTHOR

CLAWFUL

TRAP JAW

KOBRA KHAN

Laser rifle

WEBSTOR

Robotic control panel hidden under armor

FAKER

GRIZZLOR

MODULOK

Made from stinky plastic!

STINKOR

TUNG LASHOR

MANTENNA

White crossbow

HORDAK

KING HISS

Flexible rubber arms

SSSQUEEZE

Head and legs fold out from egg-shaped orb

GORE-ILLA

Packaging calls out the transformation feature

Vehicles

The original toy line included exciting vehicles alongside the action figures. These creations allowed designers to let their imaginations go wild!

Packaging art by Ruby Obrero

Missile launcher

Griffin design

Befitting the fusion of sword-and-sorcery and high-tech gadgetry that is a hallmark of the world of the Masters of the Universe, modes of transport are diverse. They range from fantasy animal steeds such as Battle Cat and Panthor to futuristic battle tanks and flyers. Later waves of toys feature hybrids of animals and machines, such as the Dragon Walker, released in 1984. Many featured exciting play features: the Dragon Walker had a motor which lets it actually walk across the floor with a figure riding on top; Skeletor's evil assault vehicle Roton featured red blades which whirl around when the vehicle is pushed forward or backward.

VEHICLE DESIGNERS

In the first year, the 20-people-strong design team at Mattel was split between Mark Taylor, who focused on the figures, and Ted Mayer, who took on the vehicles, though both worked closely together on all aspects of the line. Mayer visualized early vehicles such as Battle Ram and Wind Raider, released in 1982. He trained as an aeronautical engineer in England and, before moving to Mattel, worked as a set designer on the first *Star Wars* movie. In 2015, Mayer said, "[the Mattel team] used to go to air shows, car concourse, and hot rod shows as a group," and they put their love of cars and planes into the big wheels and exhaust pipes seen on the vehicles. Mayer enjoyed adding immense—but child-safe!—weapons and sci-fi surface details, which came easily to him after his work on *Star Wars*.

MOBILE LAUNCHER

He-Man's Battle Ram was the first vehicle released in the original toy line. Designed by Ted Mayer with input from Mark Taylor, it rolls into combat on four wheels and can split into two vehicles: the flying Sky Sled at the front and a mobile launcher at the back.

Special armor harness

Detachable jet

HEROIC SLED AND JETPACK

Designed by Ted Mayer, He-Man's heroic Jet Sled has two modes: it can attach to an action-figure's back as a jetpack and, as a hover racer, provides a flying surface to stand on.

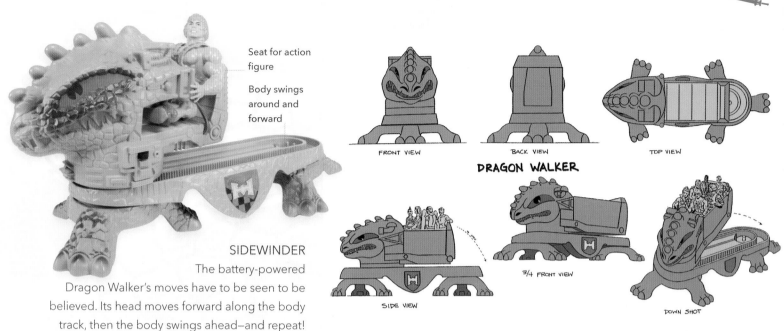

Seat for action figure

Body swings around and forward

FRONT VIEW   BACK VIEW   TOP VIEW

DRAGON WALKER

SIDE VIEW   3/4 FRONT VIEW   DOWN SHOT

SIDEWINDER

The battery-powered Dragon Walker's moves have to be seen to be believed. Its head moves forward along the body track, then the body swings ahead—and repeat!

↑ The Dragon Walker was developed for appearances in the animated cartoon.

Mouth opens for weapons storage

Rib bones hold action figures in place

DINO CARRIER

First released in 1985, Battle Bones is a beast vehicle in the shape of a dinosaur skeleton—and a useful way to carry 12 action figures on either side of the creature's spine.

Swiveling twin laser weapons

Eye stickers

Rotating blade

Grappling hook

Winder for grappling hook string

Front wheel

EVIL ASSAULT VEHICLE

Originally designed as a hero vehicle, Roton was redesigned for the Evil Warriors. When the toy is pushed forward, the red saw blade rotates around the outside of the vehicle and emits "fighting sounds" (in reality, loud clicks!).

ASSAULT LANDER

One of the first vehicles to be released, the Wind Raider became one of He-Man's signature vehicles. Its design, by Mayer and Taylor, was inspired by a sea plane and originally featured a dragon's head on the front.

Castle Grayskull

First seen in the minicomics that accompanied the toys, Castle Grayskull is the locus for the struggle between He-Man and Skeletor. A place of refuge for He-Man, Skeletor is obsessed with capturing it, believing its power will allow him to conquer Eternia and rule the Universe. Released in 1982, the impressive Castle Grayskull toy set provided the ultimate setting for playing out the struggle between the forces of good and evil. Every young fan wanted to own this awesome set, with its captivating sense of mystery, crumbling green brickwork, and ominous skull-face "Jawbridge" entrance.

FORBIDDING ARTWORK
In the box artwork, Skeletor stands on the castle's Jawbridge—with no backstory to go on at this point, artist Rudy Obrero assumed the castle was Skeletor's. Mark Taylor created the final sculpt for the castle, disappointed with the "square, English countryside-style castle" created by Mattel's sculpting team.

> "Fortress of mystery and power for He-Man and his foes."
>
> Legend on box packaging

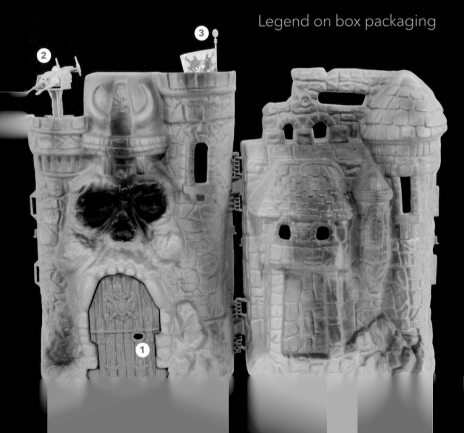

IMPOSING EXTERIOR
The Jawbridge opens when both halves of the Power Sword are inserted into a small slot on the front, like a key. At the top of the towers stands a laser cannon, for firing at invaders, and a flag, which has a hero side and a villain side, depending on who has control of the castle at that time!

CASTLE CASE:
1 Jawbridge lock
2 Laser cannon

The first floor features a weapons rack and a spinning training device. The second floor can be reached via a string-operated elevator or a movable ladder. The rug that lies in front of the throne hides a trapdoor, which can send an action figure plummeting down to the lower level, where they will land face-to-face with the dungeon grate—a sticker showing all the frightful creatures trapped in the castle's dungeon! All the artwork for the stickers (and the stickers on many other models) was done by Rebecca Taylor, Mark Taylor's wife.

1ST FLOOR: 1 Elevator **2** Gargoyle tied onto string operates pulley system for elevator **3** Ladder can be moved around **4** Training device to practice "the most powerful smack in the universe"! **5** Weapons rack with nine different weapons **6** Dungeon gra
2ND FLOOR: 7 Viewscreens **8** Suit of robot armor **9** Secret trapdoor hidden by rug **10** Throne activates trapdoor when turned

Toy Packaging

The packaging for the Masters of the Universe toy line was innovative and eye-catching, with evocative artwork and a unique additional feature: a minicomic tucked behind the toy waiting to be pored over. Mattel designer Bob Nall conceived the packaging and conceptualized the Master of the Universe logo, with its exploding red rocks and dramatic 3D-style lettering (inspired, Nall claims, by the epic block letters on the poster for the classic 1959 movie *Ben Hur*). At first, the toy line was to be named Lords of Power, but concerns that this had a religious connotation led to the switch to Masters of the Universe. Mattel's then-Marketing Director Mark Ellis came up with the idea for the minicomics in a meeting with a buyer for a toy retailer. Asked how kids would know anything about the characters without a supporting movie, Ellis told him the toys would come with comics—a first in the toy industry.

ORIGINAL ART
This piece of original art was created for the Hordak action figure released in 1985.
Hordak carries Skeletor's Havoc Staff as he and the Evil Horde storm Castle Grayskull.

DYNAMIC DESIGNS

Bob Nall design-directed the bold original packaging in conjunction with Mark Taylor. Illustrator John Hamagami created the art for the final logo, with its exploding rocks, as a 20×30-inch (60x76 cm) airbrushed painting.

GRIPPING CARDBACK

The first wave of toys in 1982 came with a cross-sell for the first eight action figures. The second wave of toys, and later rereleases of the first wave, moved to a design with 12 figures, along with a depiction of the figure's action feature and a narrative scene at the top, most of which were drawn by Mattel artist Errol McCarthy. This "12-back" design became the norm for almost all of the classic action figures from that point on.

Minicomics

The minicomics that accompanied the original action figures provided stories to help kids get to know the characters. These comics established the first lore about He-Man.

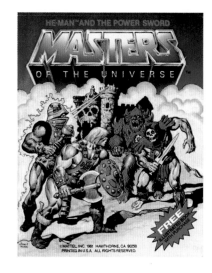

↑ Packaged with the He-Man action figure, the first comic shows He-Man leaving the jungle and clashing with Skeletor.

Created before the TV animation, the minicomics present their own version of the He-Man story. He-Man is a warrior from a jungle tribe who leaves his homelands to rid Eternia from evil forces. He wins the trust of a powerful warrior-sorcerer, Tee-La, who bequeaths him super-weapons from before the "Great War." Meanwhile, Skeletor, with his minion Beast Man, has set his sights on ancient Castle Grayskull, a fortress of mystery and power; whoever controls Grayskull will become Master of the Universe. The original four minicomics were written in 1981 by Donald F. Glut, with artwork by Alfredo Alcala.

The Power of Point Dread!/Danger at Castle Grayskull! is a 1983 comic and vinyl record audiobook.

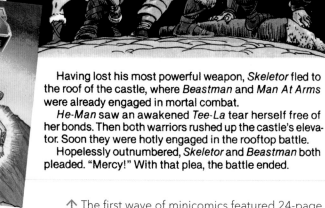

The back covers feature a cross-sell to other toys in the range.

Having lost his most powerful weapon, *Skeletor* fled to the roof of the castle, where *Beastman* and *Man At Arms* were already engaged in mortal combat.
He-Man saw an awakened *Tee-La* tear herself free of her bonds. Then both warriors rushed up the castle's elevator. Soon they were hotly engaged in the rooftop battle.
Hopelessly outnumbered, *Skeletor* and *Beastman* both pleaded. "Mercy!" With that plea, the battle ended.

↑ The first wave of minicomics featured 24-page stories that were laid out like children's picture books, with an illustration on each page and text underneath it, without speech balloons. This page comes from the first comic, *He-Man and the Power Sword*.

SECOND WAVE

Between 1982 and 1983, DC Comics created a new series of minicomics, written by Gary Cohn and featuring artwork by Mark Texeira. Now with comic-strip panels and speech balloons, these comics introduced many of the new action-figure characters in the line, such as heroes Ram Man and Man-E-Faces and villains Tri-Klops and Trap Jaw. Created before the Filmation TV series, many characters do not feature, such as Prince Adam, Cringer, Orko, and Evil-Lyn; however, the comics established characters such as a King and Queen, who would later appear in the animation, albeit looking different.

LATER MINICOMICS

With the Filmation TV series premiering in 1983, series three of the minicomics in 1984 began to feature stories and characters from it, overwriting some of the original lore. In 1985, series four began to deviate from the animation storylines and focused on new villain Hordak and the characters of the Evil Horde, who were due to appear in the animated motion picture, *He-Man and She-Ra: The Secret of the Sword.* The final two series introduced a new evil faction, the Snake Men. Led by their ancient emperor King Hiss, they rose up from Eternia's past and joined Skeletor to seek domination over Eternia. Plans were made to continue the comic series in "The Powers of Grayskull," before the toy line was discontinued.

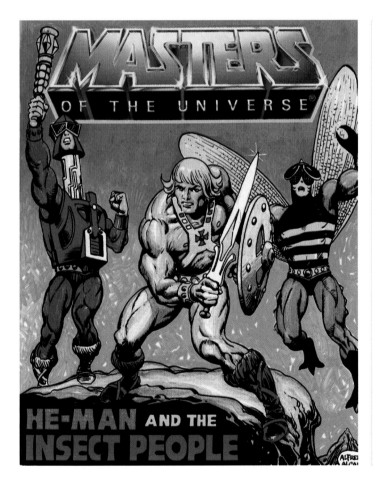

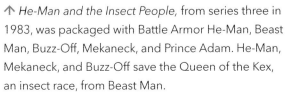

↑ *He-Man and the Insect People,* from series three in 1983, was packaged with Battle Armor He-Man, Beast Man, Buzz-Off, Mekaneck, and Prince Adam. He-Man, Mekaneck, and Buzz-Off save the Queen of the Kex, an insect race, from Beast Man.

↑ After the first wave, the minicomics were laid out as comics, with panels and speech balloons. This example comes from *The Stench of Evil!* issued in 1985 and packaged with Stinkor and Moss Man. In the comic, Moss Man must envelop himself in a shield of pure oxygen to battle noxious Stinkor!

GRIZZLOR
THE LEGEND COMES ALIVE!

-Bruce W. Timm- '84

Original layouts

← COVER LAYOUT
The cover layout shows how pasting the text onto a separate overlay allows it to be replaced for translated versions. The Masters of the Universe logo would also be swapped out for translated versions—for example, "Maitres de L'Univers" in French and "Los Amos del Universo" in Spanish.

The comic *Grizzlor—The Legend Comes Alive!* was packaged with the action figure of the hairy henchman in series four of the minicomics in 1985. The story features Hordak, the Horde, and Grizzlor, a classic horror werewolf crossed with a bear. Thought at first to be a beast of legend, Grizzlor suddenly appears very real, attacking and kidnapping Teela before He-Man and the others travel to Etheria to rescue her. The minicomics were translated in different languages, including Spanish for Mexico and various languages for Europe, including Italian, French, and German. The German/Italian versions were bilingual.

INKED PAGE
Filmation layout and background artist Bruce Timm created the inked artwork for the comic. In the 1990s, Timm became better-known for his work as co-creator and producer of *Batman: The Animated Series*.

PAGE LAYOUT
The lettering, by Stan Sakai, is pasted onto a transparent overlay. This is then photographed with the final, painted watercolor art, by Charles Simpson, ready for printing.

SC 297 | 18 | BG 289 X

TRUCK IN ON HE MANS AMAZED
EXPRESSION.

SC 298 | 3/4 FRONT UPSHOT | BG 298 | PAN
TILT FLD 2°

ROCK BEAST CHARGES FORWARD
GAINING THRU SC. SFX: ROARS

SC 299 | HE M
FROM

SC 300 | 3/4 UPSHOT 2° | BG 300 X
TILT FLD

THE ROCK BEAST APPROACHES
HE MAN WHO STANDS
READY. SFX: ROARS

SC 300A | STK·SC·6 STK | BG 2X

HE MAN THROWS A PUNCH AT

SC 300A

SC 300B | STK. | BG 289 X
ED
EN

CUT TO BACK OF ROCK
BEAST FILLING SCREEN
SFX: ROARS ABRUPTLY ENDED!

SC 300B CONT | BG

THIS EXPLODES APART IN A
SHOWER OF BOULDERS, ROCKS,
& PEBBLES.

SC 300B

LEAV
AMIDS

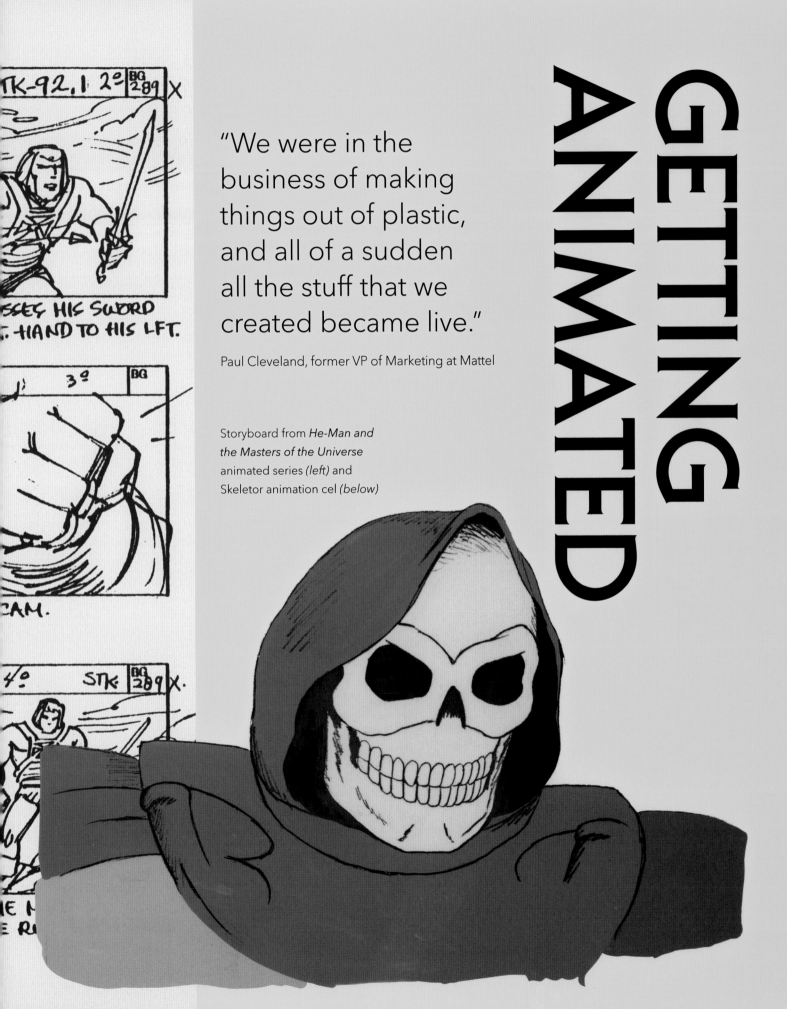

GETTING ANIMATED

"We were in the business of making things out of plastic, and all of a sudden all the stuff that we created became live."

Paul Cleveland, former VP of Marketing at Mattel

Storyboard from *He-Man and the Masters of the Universe* animated series *(left)* and Skeletor animation cel *(below)*

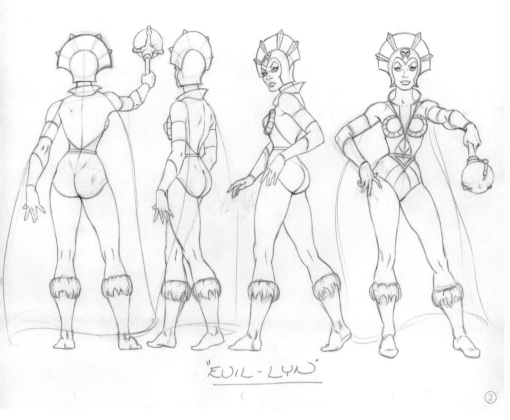

"EVIL-LYN"

① ② While scripts were written, concept drawings were made to show how characters would look and move. Evil-Lyn's headpiece here is adorned with a skull emblem that would be removed for the final animation, while Trap Jaw's robotic arm would be shortened.

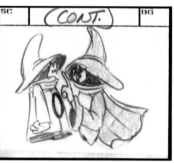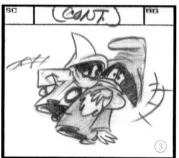

③ With scripts written and characters conceptualized, the storyboard artists got to work, turning the script into a series of comic-striplike panels. These delightful panels of Orko, drawn by Barry Caldwell, are from the storyboard for the 1984 episode, "The Return of Orko's Uncle."

9FLD

④ With the involvement of the director, layout artists work out the exact movement and framing of characters as they will appear onscreen, as a guide for the animators. Bob Kline, who had worked on many shows for Filmation, created highly expressive layouts for the episode "The Colossor Awakes" from 1983.

⑤ The soundtrack is recorded and the animators painstakingly create pencil drawings for every shot. Much animation was created specially for each episode, with stock sequences used to save time.

Developing the Animation

The incredibly popular Filmation TV animation was the moment when the Masters of the Universe went from being a hit toy line to smashing records as a billion-dollar business. He-Man really does have the power!

Pencil artwork of the Sorceress

In late 1982, Mattel approached LA-based animation production company Filmation to make an animated segment for a TV advertisement for their Castle Grayskull play set. Founded by Lou Scheimer, Norm Prescott, and Hal Sutherland in 1962, Filmation had produced many hit animated and live-action TV shows, including *Tarzan: Lord of the Jungle, Space Sentinels,* and several *New Adventures of … (Superman, Batman,* and *Flash Gordon).*

FROM PROMO TO SHOW

Heading up a team of ex-Disney animators at Filmation, animation director Gwen Wexler produced and directed the Castle Grayskull promo. So explosive and gripping was the animation that it instantly sold the full series. It was decided that the He-Man series would not be a standard Saturday morning show: it would air every weekday after school. Wexler did the calculations: her team would need to make enough half-hour shows to fill 13 weeks, a total of 65 episodes in the first season! This would mean animators working all year round.

Indeed, Mattel claimed it had a third of all the animators in Hollywood—at least 500 people—working on the show at its height.

REIMAGINED STORIES

Writer Michael Halperin wrote a "series bible" in 1982 which built on the foundation of the storylines established in the comics, tweaking and expanding the world. The animated series' story and universe centered around a reimagining of the planet Eternia. The show introduced new characters, the first being Lizard Man in the 1983 episode "She-Demon of Phantos," though he had to wait until 2015 for his action figure to appear in the Classics toy line. Caped, flying Orko was created to provide comic relief: Filmation founder and executive producer Lou Scheimer provided the voice (and many others). Most notably, the show created a more humorous persona for Skeletor, with his cackling laugh performed to perfection by voice actor Alan Oppenheimer (who also did Mer-Man, among others).

Animation Cels

In the final stage of making the animated series, artists would transfer each line drawing created by the animators onto clear acetate via Xerox. The cels would be painted on the reverse side to ensure the black line art would remain untouched. The cels were placed onto backgrounds, which had been painted separately. This highly detailed background art was used and reused with different animation cels over them. The composited images were then shot under the camera.

"We really had something special."

Lou Scheimer, Filmation president, 2006

MENACING FIGURE
An animation cel of Beast Man, with holes at the top that connect to pegs that hold each cel in place.

SNAKE MOUNTAIN
Skeletor's secret base on Eternia, Snake Mountain, is beautifully depicted in a detailed background artwork.

MAGICAL APPEARANCE
Orko hovers over a background depicting his home planet of Trolla.

I Have the Power!

The iconic opening sequence which starts each episode of the 1980s TV animation shows Prince Adam, voiced by celebrated voice actor John Erwin, introducing himself as the defender of the secrets of Castle Grayskull and acquainting us with his "fearless" friend Cringer. Then, holding aloft his sword, Adam proclaims, "By the Power of Grayskull ... I have the power!" With a planet-shaking blast of magical energy, Adam transforms into He-Man and Cringer becomes the mighty Battle Cat. Then, for good measure, He-Man throws a punch right at the camera before introducing Man-At-Arms, the Sorceress, and Orko—the only three beings who share the secret that Adam is He-Man. The stirring theme song was composed by Shuki Levy with producer (and founder of Saban Entertainment) Haim Saban. Levy composed theme songs and music for thousands of TV shows in the 1980s and 1990s, including for *She-Ra Princess of Power*.

> "The idea of being transformed into your own inner true self is very attractive."
>
> J. Michael Straczynsk, writer on *He-Man and the Masters of the Universe*

RAISED SWORD
For the scenes in which He-Man raises the Power Sword, from which He-Man's power originates, the animators created a stock sequence, which could be inserted in front of any number of backgrounds.

SWORD OF POWER

The concept for He-Man's transformation came from the early tests that Mattel's marketing team did with young children, who projected onto toys the powers they wished they had. "When He-Man says 'I have the power,'" says writer J. Michael Straczynsk, "it's saying to the kids, you don't have to do what you're told anymore; you can be your own person."

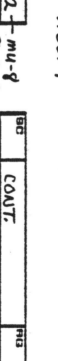

ADAM LOOKS AROUND

BG 120B   STK 76   BG 182   © POS   — MU-8 O.K.

HOLDS SWORD ALOFT

BG CONT. Start B   → PAN   © START   BG

AND REACHES FOR HIS SWORD

BG CONT.   BG

STORYBOARD

These storyboard frames show the sequence of Adam reaching for the Power Sword; the final panel shows the pan upward to the sword itself.

Grayskull Pencil

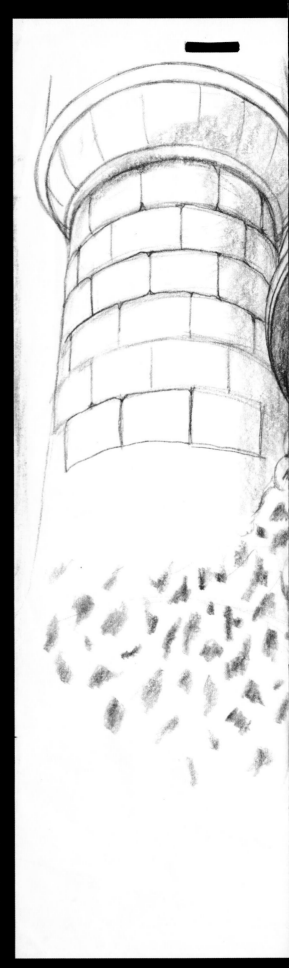

The mighty front facade of Castle Grayskull is depicted at a dramatic angle in this pencil visual for a background shot in the animated series. The finished shot would be composited with He-Man standing in front of the castle entrance, as seen in the episode "Daimar the Demon," which aired in 1984. Castle Grayskull is generally viewed from the outside in the animation, but a few interior rooms are seen, including the Throne Room, a laboratory in the basement, and the Sorceress's den.

"By the power of Grayskull,
I command the
jawbridge ... open!"

He-Man, "Daimar the Demon," 1983

PENCIL ARTWORK

Animators use a blue or red pencil for "underdrawings" because graphite (black) pencils smear; the animator then draws a final, neat version over the blue or red lines with black pencil. The blue or red pencil lines can be knocked out more easily when the final black pencil drawing is transferred via Xerox to acetate.

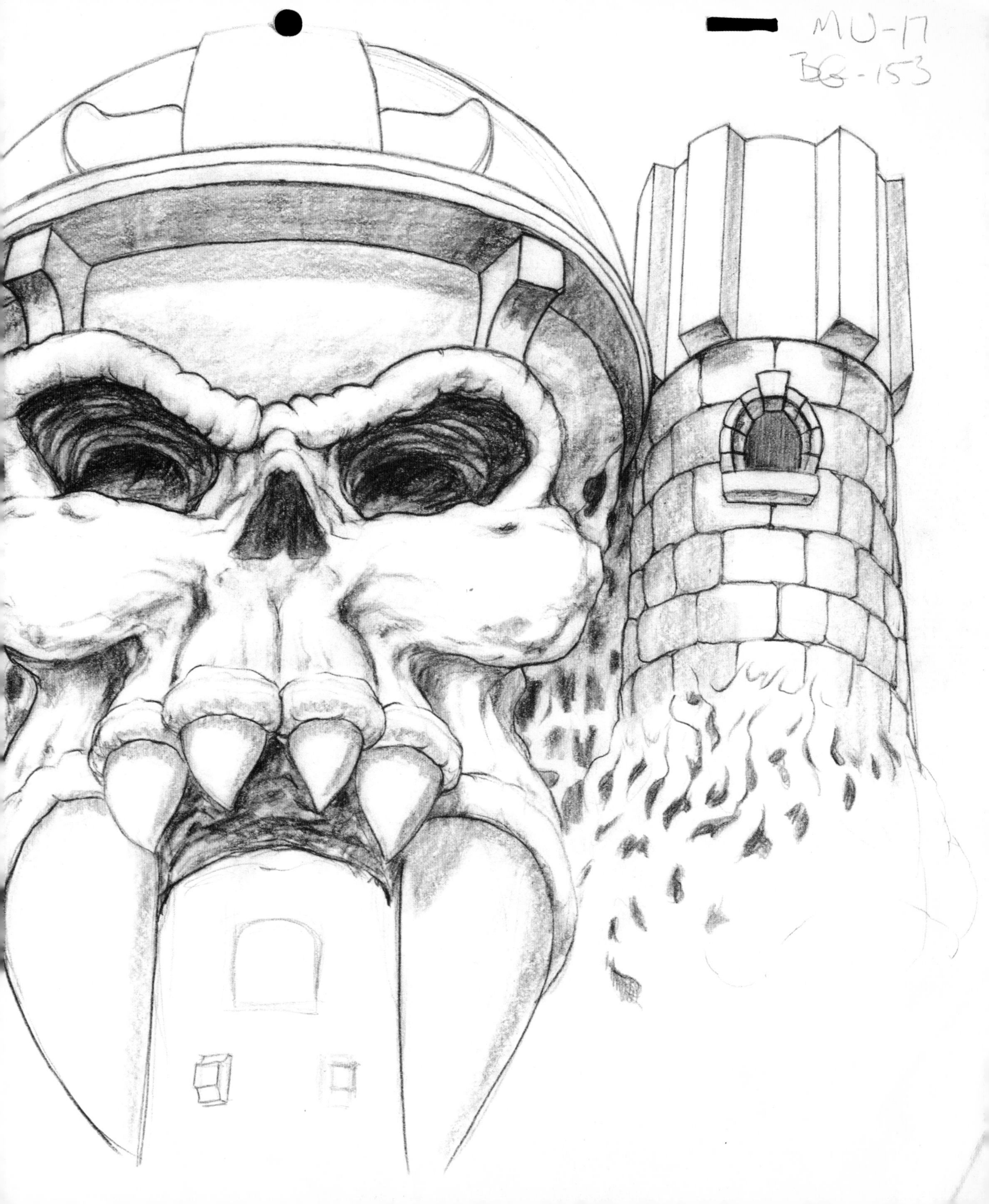
MU-17
BG-153

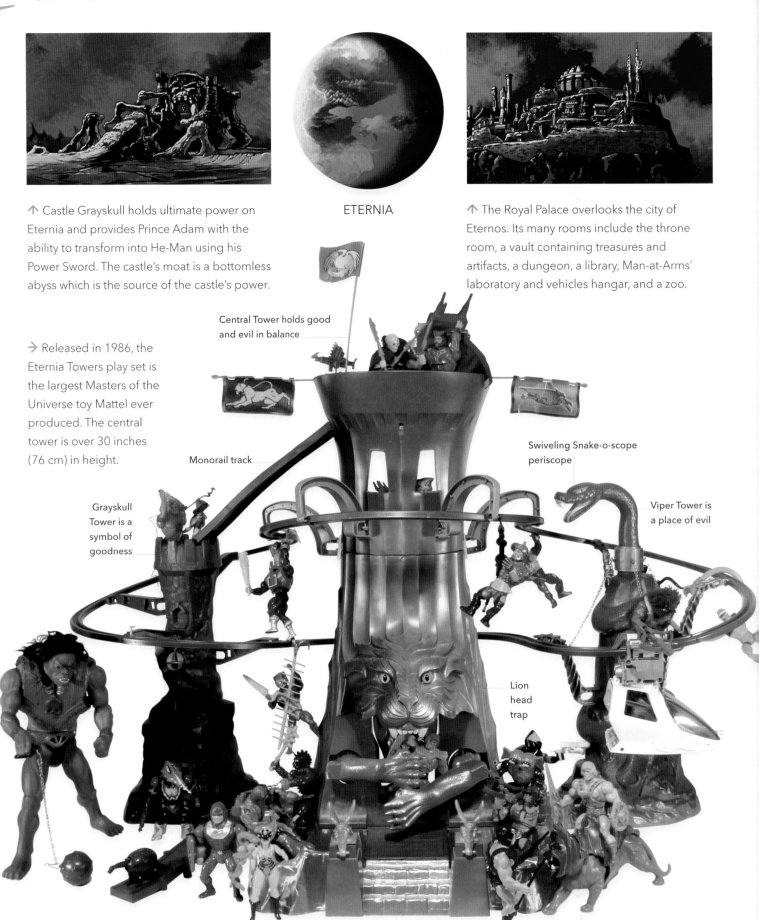

↑ Castle Grayskull holds ultimate power on Eternia and provides Prince Adam with the ability to transform into He-Man using his Power Sword. The castle's moat is a bottomless abyss which is the source of the castle's power.

ETERNIA

↑ The Royal Palace overlooks the city of Eternos. Its many rooms include the throne room, a vault containing treasures and artifacts, a dungeon, a library, Man-at-Arms' laboratory and vehicles hangar, and a zoo.

→ Released in 1986, the Eternia Towers play set is the largest Masters of the Universe toy Mattel ever produced. The central tower is over 30 inches (76 cm) in height.

Central Tower holds good and evil in balance

Monorail track

Grayskull Tower is a symbol of goodness

Swiveling Snake-o-scope periscope

Viper Tower is a place of evil

Lion head trap

Eternia

The planet Eternia is the magical world where He-Man and Skeletor battle for supremacy.

As depicted in the minicomics, the planet Eternia is a magical, beautiful, but often dangerous world devastated by long-ago wars. Barbarian tribes coexist with ferocious monsters and advanced weapons and vehicles. The mysterious Castle Grayskull stands as the focal point for the strong magical forces that exist on the planet. The ancient Eternian Elders, who ruled the planet centuries ago, foresaw danger in the future. They stored their immense powers into Castle Grayskull to aid a future champion of good.

ETERNAL BATTLEGROUND

In the Filmation animated TV series, Eternia was developed as an even more magical world, whose core is the infinitely powerful "Starseed" left over from the creation of the universe and whose position in space at a juncture of alternate universes allows magic and technology to coexist. Many races dwell on the planet, including humans, giants, Avionians (Bird People), Cat-Folk, Bee People, trolls, dragons, and many others. King Randor and Queen Marlena rule the planet from the royal palace in the capital city Eternos, where their son, Prince Adam, also resides with his cowardly pet tiger, Cringer. The planet is divided into two halves, or hemispheres: the forces of good live in the light hemisphere, while Skeletor and his Evil Warriors dominate the dark hemisphere. Skeletor inhabits the forbidding fortress of Snake Mountain, from where he schemes and plans to conquer and learn the secrets of Castle Grayskull—and to take over the royal palace and rule Eternia.

↑ Skeletor's evil stronghold, Snake Mountain, is made of pointed stone peaks with a gigantic stone snake wrapped around them. In the animated series, Skeletor constructed it himself; in the minicomics, he inherited it from King Hiss and the Snake Men, who became trapped in a pool of energy in a cavern beneath it long ago.

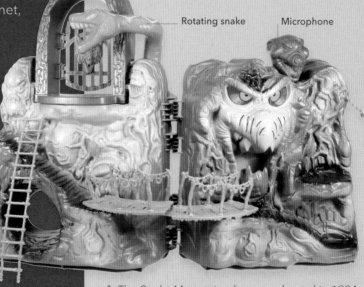

Rotating snake   Microphone

↑ The Snake Mountain play set, released in 1984, featured a built-in voice-change microphone.

He-Man

He-Man is the most powerful man in the universe—and the secret alter ego of Prince Adam.

He-Man is the muscle-bound, heroic defender of Eternia and protector of the secrets of Castle Grayskull from Skeletor and his Evil Warriors. Only a handful of people know that He-Man is the alter ego of the less-than-heroic Prince Adam: Man-At-Arms, Orko, Cringer/Battle Cat, and the Sorceress. In the earliest minicomics, He-Man was a wandering barbarian: his dual identity originated in comics created by DC Comics in 1982, with both characters in the animation voiced by the now-publicity-shy John Erwin. Filmation's president Lou Scheimer was inspired by comic-book superheroes with secret identities as ordinary teenagers: "It really empowered kids," Scheimer said. "So on He-Man, we're going from an 18-year-old kid to He-Man."

SUPERHUMAN POWERS

When Prince Adam lifts the Power Sword into the air, he transforms into He-Man, gaining incredible powers, including superhuman strength and speed—he once lifted Castle Grayskull itself, and he can pick up mountains and even move moons. He-Man's main weapons in the earlier minicomics had been his battle ax and shield, although the idea of the Power Sword being in two halves also originated in these pages; when joined, the two halves provide the key to Castle Grayskull. Restricted by broadcast guidelines, the Filmation animators avoided depicting He-Man using his sword for combat: more often, he picks villains up and throws them, or outsmarts them with his genius-level intellect!

Sword of Power can project or deflect blasts of energy

Magical chest harness enhances He-Man's strength

Fur-trimmed battle boots

↑ He-Man often uses his intellect to solve problems. "I only fight when I must," he says. "And each time, I hope it is the last time."

"When are you going to learn that evil never really can win?"

He-Man to Skeletor, "The Littlest Giant," 1984

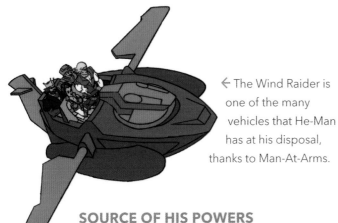

← The Wind Raider is one of the many vehicles that He-Man has at his disposal, thanks to Man-At-Arms.

SOURCE OF HIS POWERS

He-Man's powers derive from Castle Grayskull. A powerful Sorceress lives within the castle's walls, who communicates telepathically with He-Man. When Adam transforms into He-Man, his cowardly pet tiger Cringer changes into the fearless armored Battle Cat, who acts as He-Man's steed and fighting companion. Together with his allies, the Heroic Warriors, He-Man is always ready for action. As he says, "Give up, Skeletor, or we'll turn your fortress into toothpicks."

↑ He-Man wields an ax in the minicomics.

← A Prince Adam action figure was released in 1984.

↑ In a pencil sketch "The Curse of the Spellstone," Skeletor fights He-Man with a sword similar to He-Man's.

→ Whenever trouble appears, Prince Adam makes a swift exit, leaving He-Man to sort it out. As he says, "Acting like a fun-loving prince sure is hard work."

Battle Cat

Battle Cat is He-Man's heroic mount and best ally when danger strikes.

When he was a boy, Prince Adam rescued a small, green tiger cub from a sabercat in the jungle. The adopted kitten was named Cringer for his habit of cringing at any perceived dangers. The Sorceress intuited that Cringer would be useful to Prince Adam one day. After Adam gained the ability to transform himself into He-Man, he hid the secret from Cringer, not wanting to frighten him. Then, one day, he accidentally pointed his Power Sword at the cat and an energy blast shot out, making Cringer grow to twice his regular size and become adorned with red armor and a saddle. Battle Cat is fearless and talks with a commanding growl instead of Cringer's whimper. Lazy old Cringer doesn't really appreciate being changed into Battle Cat, but he accepts it out of loyalty to Adam. He largely serves as a mount for He-Man, but, if He-Man's life is in danger, he will leap into action to defend him.

↑ Young Adam carries a stray tiger cub—soon to be known as Cringer.

ORIGIN AS A TOY

Battle Cat's origins lie in the original toy line: He-Man needed a vehicle, but the team had no remaining budget. So they took an existing tiger mold from Mattel's Big Jim toy line. This tiger was much larger in scale to the He-Man action figure: horse-sized, in fact. Then-VP of Marketing Paul Cleveland suggested that artist Mark Taylor recolor the tiger green and orange and put a saddle on it, resulting in Battle Cat's final design. As Adam says in the episode "Battle Cat," "Without Battle Cat, He-Man would be a lonely fella."

↑ The Frazetta-inspired box art for the Battle Cat toy was created by artist Rudy Obrero.

↑ Mattel artist Mark Taylor created early Battle Cat concept art.

"I can't wait to get my paws on that bony creep!"

Battle Cat (about Skeletor),
"A Beastly Sideshow," 1983

↑ In the episode "The Cat And The Spider," Battle Cat teams up with Kittrina, a resourceful, talented warrior and a member of the Cat Folk.

↑ Cringer claims that the only times he doesn't feel scared are when he is eating or sleeping. He does like to talk, though: "Doesn't everybody?" he says.

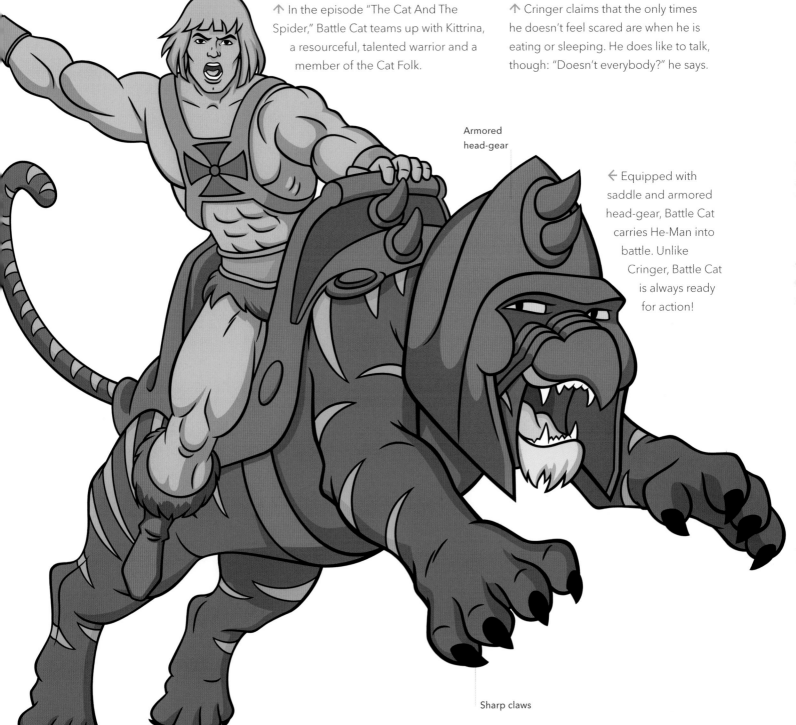

Armored head-gear

← Equipped with saddle and armored head-gear, Battle Cat carries He-Man into battle. Unlike Cringer, Battle Cat is always ready for action!

Sharp claws

Teela

A powerful and gifted fighter, Teela is a worthy Heroic Warrior.

Teela is the Captain of the Royal Guard at the palace of Eternos and a great fighter, trained in fighting skills from a young age, with a reckless streak that sometimes lands her in trouble. Unaware that Adam is He-Man, she is responsible for training and protecting him, while fighting as an equal alongside He-Man—so, when He-Man saves the day, she is often concerned about what has become of Adam and Cringer. Teela upbraids Adam for only thinking about "fun, fun, fun," though she reluctantly admits to appreciating his wit, and admires He-Man's courage. (If only they could be one person!)

FAMILY SECRETS

Teela is Man-At-Arms' adopted daughter. In the episode "Teela's Quest," she discovers that her mother is the Sorceress. The Sorceress informs Teela that one day she will take her place as the guardian of Grayskull. However, at the end of the episode, the Sorceress—reluctantly—erases the memory from Teela's mind, believing her to be safer not knowing. Of her birth father, Teela only knows from Man-At-Arms that he was a great man who gave his life in battle to protect Eternia.

A WARRIOR BORN AND BRED

Teela was one of the first characters developed for Masters of the Universe. In the minicomics, she is a blonde-haired, unicorn-riding "warrior goddess," who possesses "the spirits of many ancestral champions." Her action figure, released in the second half of the first wave, features the cobra

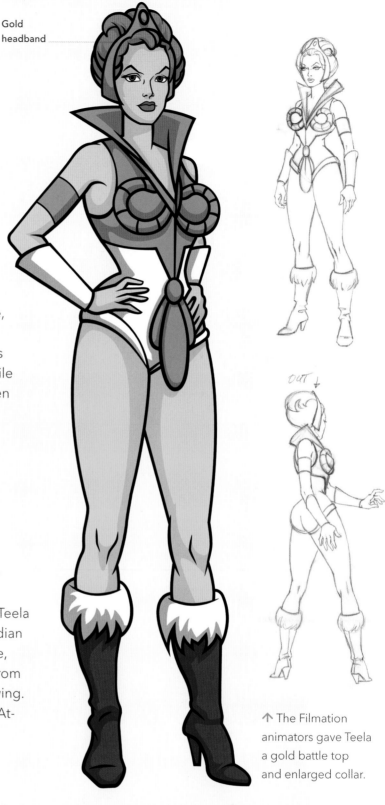

Gold headband

↑ The Filmation animators gave Teela a gold battle top and enlarged collar.

OUT ↓

hood and cobra staff developed in early concept art—with them, she is the Goddess; without them, she is the warrior Teela. Eventually, the Goddess role shifted to the Sorceress and in the animated series and the comics, Teela appears with neither cobra hood or staff.

← In the earliest minicomics, Teela is a blonde-haired "warrior goddess" who battles like a demon against Skeletor and Beast Man.

↓ In the animated series, Teela goes into battle with her sword.

← Artist Rudy Obrero created unique packaging art for a gift set of Teela and Zoar, released in 1983 before the Filmation animation started. Zoar is not yet the Sorceress and Teela is still depicted in her early incarnation as a warrior goddess.

"This whole thing smells of Skeletor."

Teela to He-Man, "Day of the Machines," 1984

← Teela and the Sorceress share a close bond. "I never knew my mother," Teela says to the Sorceress, "but I wish she could be just like you."

King Randor

King Randor is the heroic ruler of Eternia.

The early minicomics depicted an elderly, unnamed king with a long white beard. He and the Queen ruled an Eternian kingdom while sending the Heroic Warriors on missions. In an intriguing story twist in the minicomics, the writers hinted that Randor had a long-lost brother, Keldor—who became Skeletor! In the TV animation, King Randor is a middle-aged man whose goal is for a united and peaceful universe—starting with Eternia. Randor has no idea that his son Prince Adam is He-Man; he just thinks he's a lazy, good-for-nothing layabout (though he loves him). Randor returns in *The New Adventures of He-Man* in 1990 and plays a more active role in the 2002 animated series, continuing to live by his motto: "Never give up!"

↑ King Randor gets animated with his scepter, in animation sketches.

Removable chest armor and cloak

Royal staff of Eternia

↑ King Randor's muscle-bound action figure was released in 1986.

↑ In the minicomics, Randor is older than he is in the animated series.

↑ In the animation, Randor is a wise king rather than an action hero.

Queen Marlena

Queen Marlena is an ace pilot who knows how to take charge in a crisis.

→ Marlena enjoys action and adventure—royal life is sometimes too calm for her.

In the animated series, Marlena Glenn, voiced by Linda Gary, is a pioneer female astronaut from the planet Earth. When her spaceship, the *Rainbow Explorer*, crashed on Eternia, the first person she met was King Randor—and she decided to stay. They married and had twins, Adam and Adora. Marlena once borrowed her now-repaired spaceship from its museum storage to defeat an attempt by Skeletor to take over the palace. She also helped save Castle Grayskull when Skeletor tried to destroy it with a missile from her home planet Earth.

A MOTHER KNOWS

Marlena is less judgmental than her husband of their son Adam's carefree nature—she occasionally hints that she knows his secret. "A mother always knows her own son," she tells Adam in the episode "The Rainbow Warrior," "... and what he is capable of doing." The 2002 animated series develops Marlena's character further, sending her on diplomatic missions around Eternia.

← Marlena, in a pencil sketch from the TV animation.

↑ Marlena and Randor make battle plans in a layout drawing from the episode "Teela's Trial."

← A younger Marlena freshly landed on Eternia from Earth, from the 1984 episode "The Rainbow Warrior."

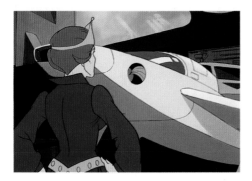

↑ Queen Marlena views her ship, the *Rainbow Warrior*, in its museum storage.

The Sorceress

The powerful and mysterious Sorceress is the guardian of Castle Grayskull and the protector of Eternia.

↑ In the first minicomics, the Sorceress wears the cobra-themed armor that will become Teela's in comics and toys.

In the classic minicomics, the Sorceress—also referred to as the Goddess—is a green-skinned, magical figure who instructs He-Man to protect Castle Grayskull. She entrusted He-Man with the guardianship of the Power Sword and also gave him high-tech armor, vehicles, and weaponry that dated from before the "Great War." The minicomics also relate how Skeletor magically creates a child clone of the Sorceress, who Man-At-Arms raises as his own child and calls Teela—for the real name of the Sorceress.

POWERFUL PRESENCE

In the animated series, the Sorceress was a peasant girl, Teela Na, who sought refuge in Castle Grayskull and was magically transformed into its guardian. Years later, the Sorceress had a daughter, Teela, who Man-At-Arms raised as his own to help keep her safe. The Sorceress lives alone within Castle Grayskull, where her magical powers are strongest, talking within the castle only with the ghostly Spirit of Grayskull. She also communicates telepathically with He-Man and Teela. The Sorceress can cast spells, teleport herself and others across huge distances, disguise herself as other people, and produce magical shields. When she needs to venture outside the castle, she often transforms into a mighty falcon, Zoar. Selflessly, the Sorceress looks over the people of Eternia and guards the secrets of the castle.

↑ The Sorceress is a wise being who offers advice and support to many people, including He-Man. Her powers weaken when she leaves Castle Grayskull, except when she transforms into her falcon form.

Falcon headdress

Ball-joined arms

Magical staff

"Only here at Grayskull are my powers strong enough to combat Skeletor."

The Sorceress, "The Mystery of Man-E-Faces," 1983

← The Sorceress's action figure is issued in 1986, toward the end of the line. The spring-loaded wings pop up when the tail feature is pressed.

↑ In the animated series, Zoar has orange, blue, and white feathers, which reflect the look of the Sorceress.

→ In the animated episode, "Dragon Invasion," Skeletor traps the Sorceress inside a powerful Dragonpearl, allowing him to put a forcefield around Castle Grayskull.

Man-At-Arms

Man-At-Arms is a master of weapons, a mentor to He-Man, and the adoptive father of Teela.

Duncan, known as Man-At-Arms, advises the royal leaders of Eternia and leads the Royal Guard. He is a soldier and a skillful inventor and repairer of vehicles, weapons, and machines, with his own laboratory in the palace. Man-At-Arms is Teela's foster father. He agreed to look after Teela as a baby when her mother, the Sorceress, feared that Castle Grayskull was too dangerous. "She will always be safe with me for as long as I live," Man-At-Arms vowed. To Prince Adam, Man-At-Arms is a mentor and almost a second father—he is often more understanding of the Prince than Adam's own father, King Randor. Irritated when Orko's tricks backfire on him, Man-At-Arms quickly forgives: "I'm sure if it weren't for Orko," he says, "I never would've learned to laugh at myself." Man-At-Arms is among the few people who know He-Man's secret identity. He also knows that Adam's twin sister Adora is She-Ra.

WEAPONS MASTER

Man-At-Arms will continue to be developed as the franchise moves into the 2000s, with the 2002 animated cartoon showing new sides to him, from his deeper connection with the Sorceress to giving him a brother, Fisto, and a mentor named Dekker. Jumping Jupiter! Man-At-Arms always comes through!

Cybernetic helmet

Mace

→ Man-At-Arms wears a high-tech suit of armor—and, in the Filmation animation, a mustache, which the earlier toy did not have; the animators wanted him to look more fatherly.

WE RIDE TO FIND TEELA, GOOD MAN-AT-ARMS! BUT WHY DO YOU HOLD BACK?

I MUST STAY BEHIND, MY FRIEND--TO PURSUE *ANOTHER PATH!*

AND AFTER THEY DEPART...

HO, NOBLE MAN-AT-ARMS! I SENSED THAT I AM *NEEDED* HERE!

AYE, GODDESS...FOR THOUGH HE-MAN IS ETERNIA'S *MIGHTIEST HERO,* AND HIS FRIENDS BE BRAVE AND TRUE, I FEAR IT IS *WE* WHO MUST SAVE MY DAUGHTER!

↑ In the minicomics, Man-At-Arms' people are well-known in Eternia as weapons masters.

Computer screen control panel

← Man-At-Arms' computer-powered hover-chair can control everything from a small drill to the palace defenses.

← Man-At-Arms' outfit was inspired by armor of Spanish conquistadors.

"Keep back, you overgrown garden pest!"

Man-At-Arms to Beast Man, "The Song of Celice," 1983

Orko

Orko is a floating, blue court jester—and an unreliable wizard!

O rko hails from the extradimensional world of Trolla, where custom dictates the hiding of one's face. Consequently, this flying being is almost completely hidden beneath his robe, hat, and scarf. On his home world, Orko is an accomplished wizard known as "Orko the Great," but on Eternia his magical skills are ... unreliable. His attempts to provide entertainment at the court generally backfire—often against Man-At-Arms, whose lab he sometimes disrupts as well. One aspect of Orko's magic is always reliable, though: his ability to store an infinite number of items inside his hat!

Hat and scarf hide face

"Dee la ka, dee la ra, dee la vee!"

Orko casts a spell, "Orko's Return," 1987

↑ Childlike, innocent, and humorous, Orko loves showing off his magic tricks, despite frequent mishaps. He can teleport himself when he needs to, though!

12FC

①

← Artist Bruce Timm drew this pencil sketch of Orko for the episode "A Beastly Sideshow" from 1983.

↑ In "Orko's Return," Beast Man and Trap Jaw kidnap Orko. The Trollan torments his captors with magic tricks until they are glad to get rid of him!

SC-127
BG-127
STK 102A

Trollan hood

↑ Orko has a relationship with another Trollan named Dree Elle. As is traditional in Trolla, they show their faces to each other to signify their love.

SC 75 | REF 65 | BG 75

ORKO
(to Montork)
Good! Wait till you see me in action, Uncle Montork!

SC | (CONT.) | BG

ORKO
My magic's really super good now!

SC | (CONT.) | BG

MONTORK
Fine, Orko, fine. But just be careful. Azrog and Spydra are a dangerous pair!

SC | (CONT.) | BG

ORKO
Well, they'd better watch out for me and my uncle!

↑ Orko's Uncle Montork, seen in a storyboard from "The Return of Orko's Uncle" from 1984, is head of the Trollan Academy of Magic and taught Orko everything he knows.

Removable hat

"Magic" coins with printed stickers

↑ Orko's toy came with small plastic coins which "magically" change from Evil to Heroic Warriors.

UNEXPECTED ARRIVAL

Orko arrived in Eternia by accident during a season of cosmic storms on his planet. He meets Adam and Cringer and rescues them from a tar pit. King Randor makes him a member of the royal court as a reward for saving his son. Orko becomes one of Adam's closest friends—and one of the few people who know that Adam is secretly He-Man. Despite his timid nature, the Trollan is always ready to help his friends.

SPECIAL CHARACTER

Orko was created specially for the Filmation animation. He was Filmation president Lou Scheimer's favorite character; he voiced Orko himself. Initially, Orko was named Gorpo, but with an "O" on his shirt instead of a "G," he could be more easily flipped, making life easier for the animators. Orko's toy, from 1984, includes a ripcord feature which allows it to move around in circles.

Great Heroes

He-Man leads the Heroic Warriors, a loosely organized group of heroes who defend the kingdom of Eternia and Castle Grayskull against Skeletor and other evildoers. Most Heroic Warriors possess superhuman abilities and unique talents. First appearing in the 1980s toy line, many of the Heroic Warriors' stories were established in the minicomics that came with the toys. In the 1980s, many of them were further developed in the animated TV series and in comics and books.

Monster face

Image created for original film cel

MAN-E-FACES
Eternia's greatest actor, Man-E-Faces can transform his face and personality from man to monster to robot. Though he is loyal to the Heroic Warriors, Skeletor has made attempts to control his monster personality.

"Eyyy guys, when you got it, you got it!"

Ram Man, "Wizard of Stone Mountain," 1983

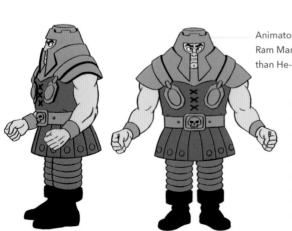

Animators made Ram Man shorter than He-Man

Ax accessory

RAM MAN
With legs made of spring coils, Ram Man has the powers of a human battering ram. In the minicomics and animated series, he is somewhat dim-witted and comical—he sometimes rams himself into unconsciousness!

Spring-loaded torso for "ramming" action feature

FISTO

With his mighty fist, Fisto's fighting power is nearly a match for He-Man's. Initially an ally of Skeletor, Fisto switches sides after his life is saved in Eternia and he joins the Heroic Warriors.

Sword gripped by left hand

Fist with giant knuckles

Body based on He-Man mold

MEKANECK

Man-At-Arms rescues a man who sustains a neck injury in a storm on Dragon Mountain. He equips the man with a bionic, extending neck. Now known as Mekaneck, this Heroic Warrior often works with Buzz-Off on scout and spying missions.

Visor for long-distance sight

STRATOS

One of the original eight action figures, Stratos is the Heroic Warriors' winged warrior. His natural powers of flight are enhanced by the jetpack he wears. In the animation, his power derives from the Egg of Avion and he can fire blasts from his hands and beams of light from his wrist cuffs.

ZODAC

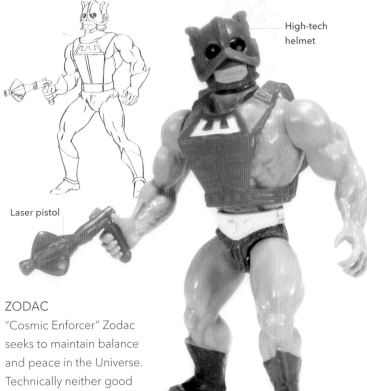

High-tech helmet

Laser pistol

"Cosmic Enforcer" Zodac seeks to maintain balance and peace in the Universe. Technically neither good nor evil, he tends more toward the side of good.

Unbeatable Warriors

He-Man's Heroic Warriors welcome new recruits to help them in the eternal battle against Skeletor and his Evil Warriors. Some, such as Roboto, arrive on Eternia from other worlds, while others, such as Buzz-Off, become helpful allies while also remaining loyal to their own nation of beings. Each of these warriors has special skills and powers, which makes this team of heroes unbeatable!

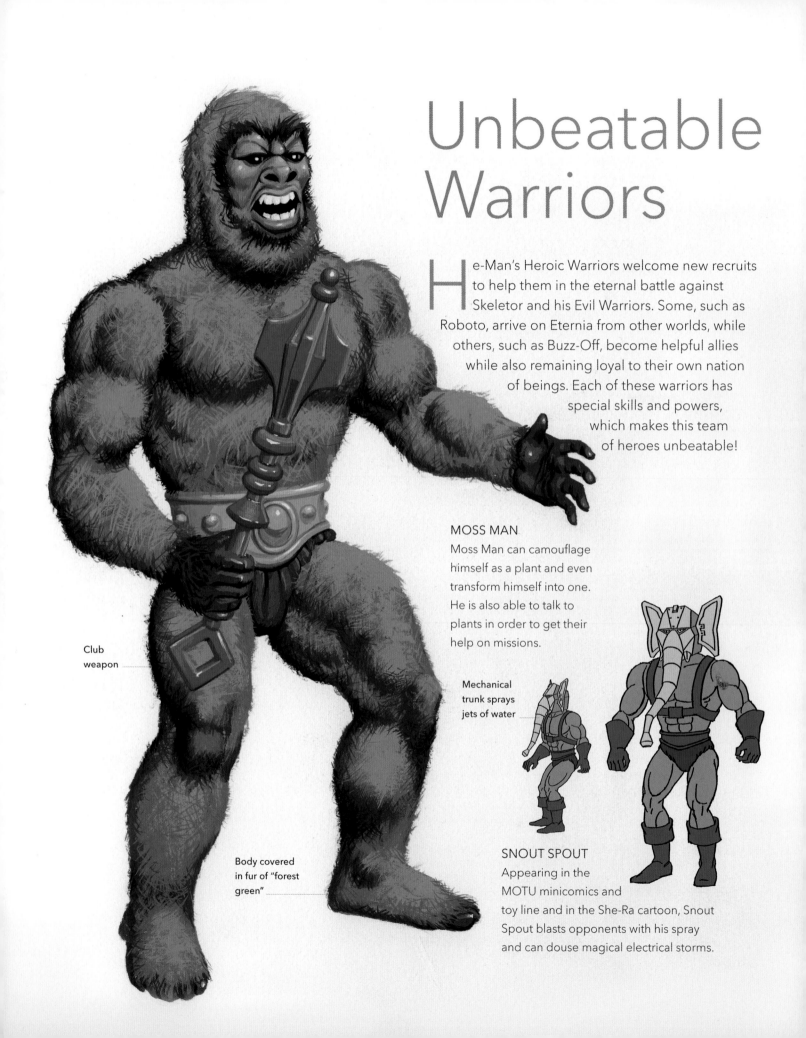

Club weapon

Body covered in fur of "forest green"

MOSS MAN
Moss Man can camouflage himself as a plant and even transform himself into one. He is also able to talk to plants in order to get their help on missions.

Mechanical trunk sprays jets of water

SNOUT SPOUT
Appearing in the MOTU minicomics and toy line and in the She-Ra cartoon, Snout Spout blasts opponents with his spray and can douse magical electrical storms.

Helmet with second
pair of eyes

Translucent
yellow wings

BUZZ-OFF

As well as being a Heroic Warrior,
Buzz-Off is the leader of the Bee People
on Eternia. Often paired with Mekaneck,
he uses his X-ray vision goggles to see
across great distances and typically
carries an ax in his clawed hand.

Laser
attachment

Translucent torso

ROBOTO

Mechanical warrior
Roboto crashed onto
Eternia from the planet
Robotica. Man-At-
Arms repaired him
and he joined the
Heroic Warriors.

Shiny
silver
boots

SY-KLONE

The blue-faced human tornado
Sy-Klone flies by rotating his arms
at high speed. His spinning arms
can also create enemy-
repelling gusts of wind.

Radar
screen
on chest

Arms fly upward
when spinning

Green skin
(sometimes
shown as
brown)

Radar
plots flight
courses

LIZARD MAN

Voiced by Lou Scheimer, Lizard Man
appeared infrequently in the animated
series and as an action figure only in 2015. Aiding
the Heroic Warriors, he can leap great heights
and stick to walls. He is also known to enjoy
sunbathing on large, flat rocks.

Planetary
red rings

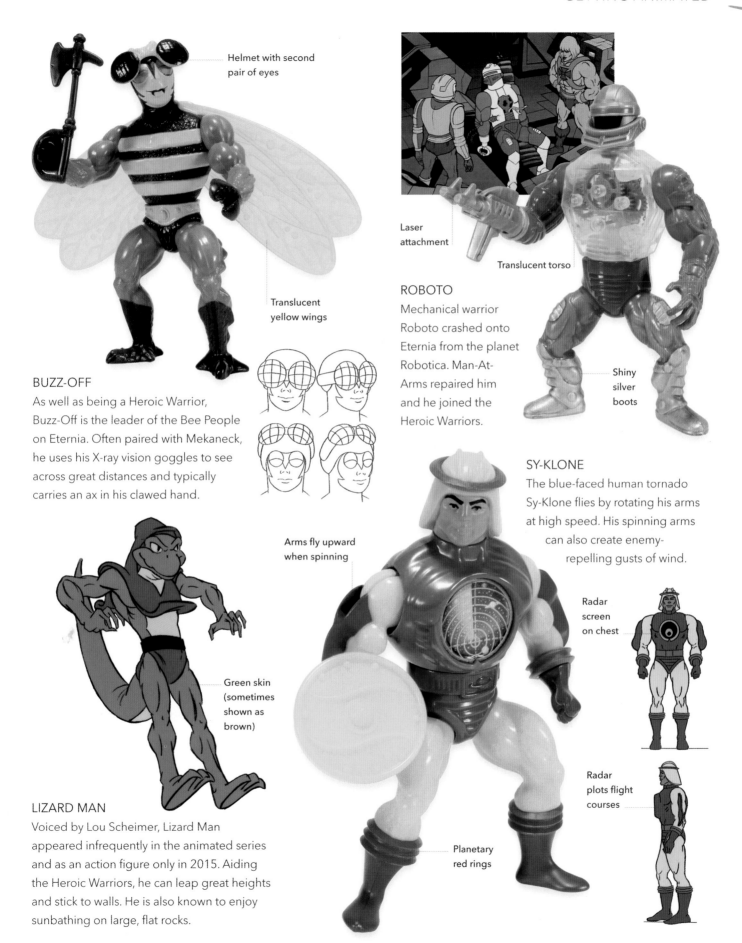

"Today, I want to talk to you about courage. Now, courage not only means being brave in the face of danger, it also means having the strength to say no when your friends are trying to talk you into doing something you know is wrong."

He-Man, "A Beastly Sideshow"

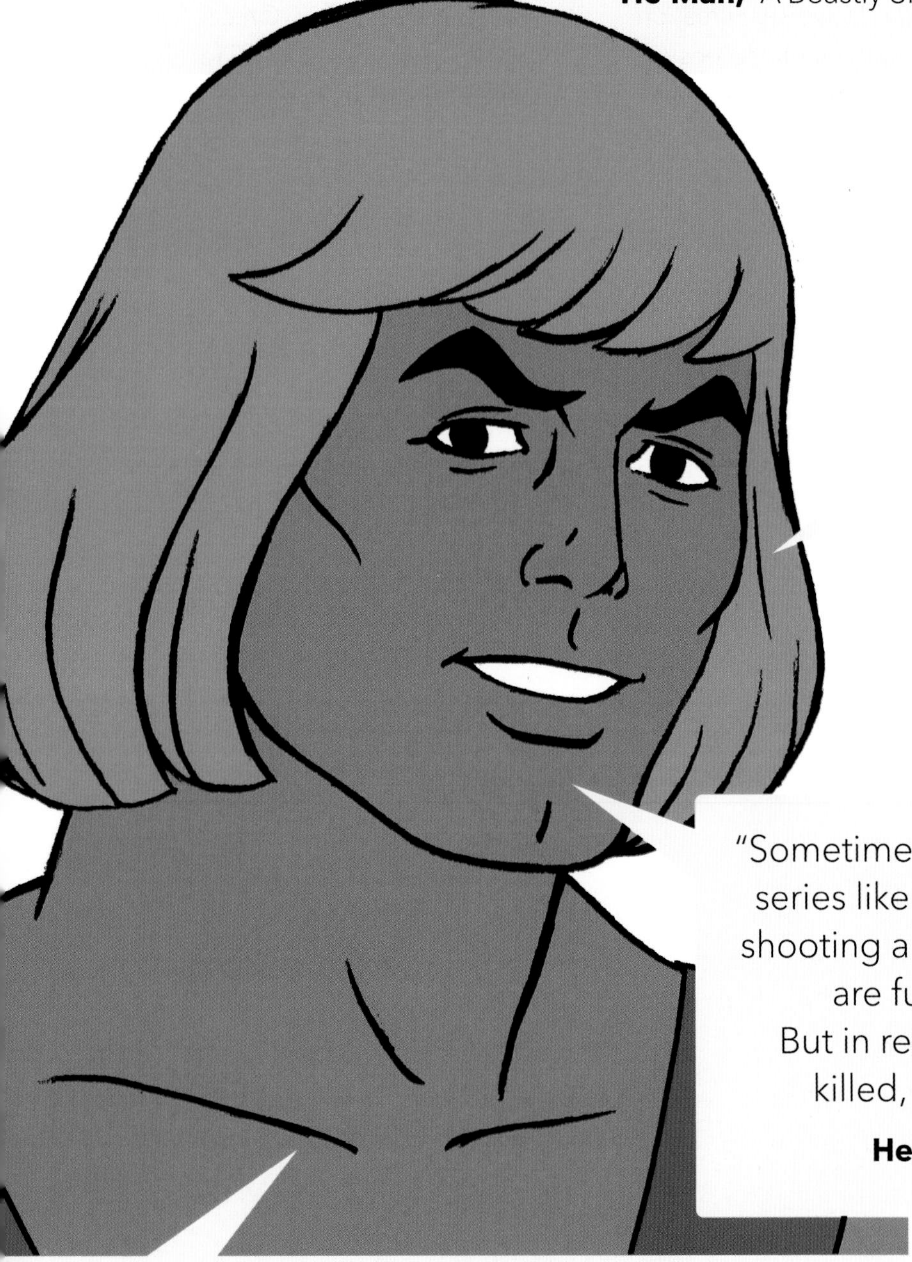

"I hope you enjoyed today's adventure. You know television is not the only way to be entertained by an exciting story. There is another way; it's called reading."

He-Man, "A Tale of Two Cities"

"Sometimes movies and television adventure series like this one make it seem as though shooting a gun, fighting, and taking chances are fun and exciting things to do. But in real life, people do get hurt, even killed, when they fight or use guns."

He-Man, "Double Edged Sword"

"Today's story was about something more precious, more valuable than gold or silver. It's called friendship."

Adam, "Creatures From The Tar Swamp"

In Today's Story

Since the late 1960s, children's television in the US had been strictly regulated to reduce the exposure of children to violence and advertising. However, in 1981, President Ronald Reagan brought in deregulation, which led to the debut of many toy-focused series,

including *He-Man and the Masters of the Universe*. Filmation and Mattel were careful to ensure that violence in the show was kept to a minimum: He-Man rarely used his sword or his fists, preferring to brain-box or wrestle with his opponents. In addition, to assuage criticism or parental

disapproval, each episode concluded with He-Man, Orko, Teela, and others offering a "life lesson" or "moral of the story." Written by the show's staff writers rather than the script writers, these wise words were a commentary on the plot or central theme of that episode.

"Never take drugs from other people. Even if a close friend says it's all right, check with someone who really loves you. See you next time."

Teela, "The Eternia Flower"

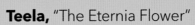

"You should never judge a person by the way he looks, but rather by the way he behaves."

Man-At-Arms, "City Beneath the Sea"

"Ramming things may look like fun, but it really isn't. Trying to use your head the way I do is not only dangerous, it's dumb."

Ram Man, "House of Shokoti" Part 1

"In today's story, Skeletor tried to conquer Eternia by using animals in an evil way. Animals, like all living things, should be treated with kindness and respect."

Orko, "The Dragon Invasion"

Skeletor

Skeletor is the evil lord of destruction and He-Man's arch foe. He will not rest until he rules the entire universe!

← Battle Armor Skeletor, released in 1984, shows "battle damage" when his chest plate is hit.

S ince his first appearance in the original toy line and minicomics that accompanied them, the maniacally grinning figure of Skeletor has been a constant malevolent presence in the world of the Masters of the Universe. With his hooded skull-face and purple robes, this muscle-bound fiend has been intent on defeating He-Man and capturing Castle Grayskull—believing its mysterious power would allow him to conquer Eternia and rule the universe. Armed with his Havoc Staff, a magical weapon topped with a ram's skull, Skeletor wields dark powers of sorcery. He can teleport himself across huge distances and fire energy bolts from his fingertips. He rides into battle on Panthor, a giant purple panther, who otherwise lurks beside Skeletor's throne. Yet, throughout the 1980s cartoon series and beyond, He-Man and the Masters of the Universe repeatedly foil Skeletor's evil plans. Sometimes, this is because Skeletor lets his anger or hubris get the better of him; most often, his bumbling minions let him down: "Why do I surround myself with fools?" Skeletor groans.

↓ Skeletor's appearances in the 1980s TV series were voiced by veteran voice actor Alan Oppenheimer.

Havoc Staff

Purple battle harness

MYSTERIOUS ORIGINS

Over the decades, Skeletor's origins have evolved and changed. In the minicomics that accompanied the first wave of toys, he burst into Eternia from another dimension, then planned to harness the power of Castle Grayskull to lead his race in a large-scale invasion. By the time of the animated series in the 1980s, Skeletor had been betrayed by his mentor, Hordak, the leader of an army of savage warriors known as the Evil Horde.

Abandoned on Eternia, Skeletor took up residence in Snake Mountain and raised an army of minions to gain control of Eternia and avenge himself against Hordak. In later retellings, Skeletor is He-Man's uncle Keldor, the long-lost brother (or possibly half-brother) of King Randor. Keldor's dangerous experiments in magic transported him to a "dimension beyond time," from which he returns as Skeletor. This all-time classic villain has proved he still has plenty of surprises up his purple sleeves to please his fans!

ARCH ENEMIES

Only one man stands in the way of Skeletor's plans for total domination: He-Man. Being the most powerful man in the universe, He-Man is a formidable foe and Skeletor must draw on all his skills to do battle with him: not only his magical powers, but also his cunning intellect and ability to create devious machines and devices. Knowing that He-Man's power resides in his Power Sword, Skeletor aims to possess it. In the early Mattel toys and minicomics, the sword is in two halves, one half of which is held by Skeletor and the other by He-Man: only by possessing both halves can the complete sword be created, allowing total power! But although He-Man always wins, Skeletor has the best lines: he is a master of the insult. His minions are "wimps" and "pathetic pinheads"; King Randor is a "royal boob"; and He-Man is a "muscle-bound oaf" or, simply, "muscle-boy." Skeletor never gives up. As he says, "Everything comes to he who waits … I'll be back!"

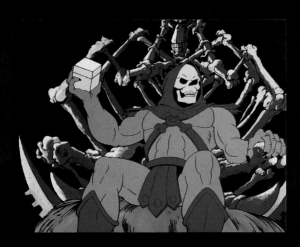

↑ Skeletor sits on his bone throne in his sinister base of operations, Snake Mountain.

SKELETOR'S HAVOC STAFF

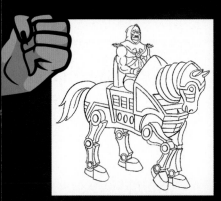

← Skeletor's robotic horse Nightstalker, shown in a pencil sketch from the animated series.

↑ This detailed pencil sketch for the animated series shows designs for Skeletor's Havoc Staff.

"We'll win this game the old-fashioned way, the tried and true way: we'll cheat!"

Skeletor, "The Games," 1985

LETHAL LABORATORY

A large curved area forms part of Skeletor's laboratory. On the right of the image, the glass window, with an instruments panel below it, looks into a room where Skeletor stores new experimental weapons.

SKELETOR'S VAULTS

Beautifully detailed background art shows a vault within Snake Mountain. The hole that He-Man punched in the exterior wall can be seen on the left, and the large metal door he crumples up like paper is on the the right.

STOP SKELETORS LAB

MU-52
BG-15?

Skeletor's Lair

In the 1985 episode "Teela's Trial," Trap Jaw captures Man-At-Arms and Skeletor locks him in one of his dungeons in Snake Mountain. He-Man and Teela arrive to rescue him, with He-Man trying the "simple and direct" way of gaining entry: He punches his way through an exterior wall with his bare fists, emerging into one of Skeletor's vaults. Filmation artists visualized these locations within Snake Mountain in incredibly detailed concept art, with jagged spikes around doorways and surfaces covered with technical-looking details, known as "greebles" in the film industry. The concept art was transcribed faithfully into color background painting and used for several panning shots in the episode. These locations would appear again numerous times.

Evil-Lyn

No mere minion, the dark sorceress Evil-Lyn only deigns to work for Skeletor because she wishes to acquire his ultimate powers.

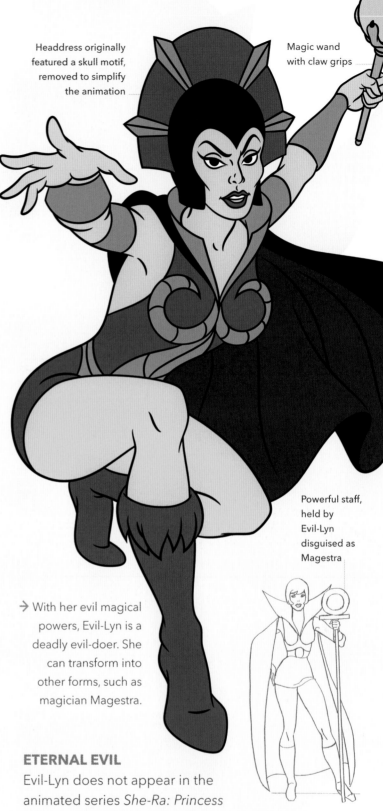

Headdress originally featured a skull motif, removed to simplify the animation

Magic wand with claw grips

Powerful staff, held by Evil-Lyn disguised as Magestra

→ With her evil magical powers, Evil-Lyn is a deadly evil-doer. She can transform into other forms, such as magician Magestra.

With her intellect, bravery, and incredible powers of sorcery, Evil-Lyn is vastly more capable—and downright stylish—than the rest of Skeletor's Evil Warriors. She operates as the Evil Lord's second-in-command and often deputizes for him when he leaves Snake Mountain. But Evil-Lyn sometimes also works independently of her boss, recruiting other Evil Warriors or teaming up with super-villains instead of Skeletor. Voice actor Linda Gary gave the character the perfect blend of evil cunning and cutting wit: "Do you think I can do nothing without Skeletor?" she would shout at other Evil Warriors. "Ha! Think again!"

MAGIC POWERS

Though described as an "evil warrior goddess" on her toy packaging, Evil-Lyn is not a physical fighter. Initially, she was intended to be an evil version of Teela—they share the same body mold for their classic 1980s action figures and match each other for strong, independent personalities. But Evil-Lyn's powers are of magic and witchcraft, making her more of an evil counterpart to the Sorceress. She casts many spells in her battles with the Heroic Warriors, transforming them into animals and stone—or worse—and uses magic to disguise herself. She can also blast magic beams from her eyes or hands and can turn herself into a fireball when she wants to make a hasty exit.

ETERNAL EVIL

Evil-Lyn does not appear in the animated series *She-Ra: Princess of Power*, but she gets up to her old power-hungry and deceitful ways in the 1987 feature film, the 2002 animated series, and beyond. No one, not even Skeletor, can contain her! "Evil-Lyn, what do you want?" barks Skeletor, to which the evil witch calmly replies, "Your power, Skeletor—HA HA HA!"

"I have no loyalty to Skeletor. It's his power I want!"

Evil-Lyn, "The Witch and the Warrior," 1983

→ Evil-Lyn reveals her cropped hair in a pencil drawing from the episode "The Witch and the Warrior."

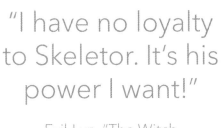

← "And so, He-Man, those great, gorgeous muscles of yours are totally useless," taunts Evil-Lyn about a trap she has constructed.

Headdress with skull motif, shown in animation sketch

→ In some of her appearances in the minicomics, Evil-Lyn has yellow skin, similar to her action figure.

BUT AT SNAKE MOUNTAIN, DARK PLANS ARE ALREADY BREWING!

HA! GRAY-SKULL STANDS UNPROTECTED! HOW LONG I HAVE WAITED TO REIGN AS ETERNIA'S MOST EVIL QUEEN!

YET SKELETOR HAS NOT THE STRENGTH TO TAKE THE CASTLE!

HE HAS FAILED SO MANY TIMES!

COULD IT BE THAT ONLY HORDAK HAS THE POWER TO FULFILL MY DARK DESIRES?

SLIPPING AWAY FROM SNAKE MOUNTAIN, EVIL-LYN MAKES HER WAY TO THE PORTAL TO...

2

Beast Man

Skeletor often unleashes his savage henchman Beast Man to destroy He-Man.

One of the first four toys to be issued—along with He-Man, Man-At-Arms, and Skeletor—Beast Man is Skeletor's right-hand beast. Ferocious and deadly, Beast Man has the power to summon and control wild creatures from across Eternia to assist in Skeletor's evil plots—though, as Teela notes, Skeletor controls Beast Man, despite his attempts to talk back to his master. Beast Man appeared in the first minicomic, "He-Man and the Power Sword," and the first-ever cartoon episode, "Diamond Ray of Disappearance." He becomes a regular character and often teams up with Trap Jaw. Beast Man's backstory is mysterious: According to the animation story bible, he came from Earth and was mutated into Beast Man; elsewhere, he comes from a tribe of jungle-dwelling Beast People. In the *Masters of the Universe* feature film in 1987, he becomes "The Beastman," and he has been reinvented for every new toy line and animation since. He's not the "King of Beasts" for nothing!

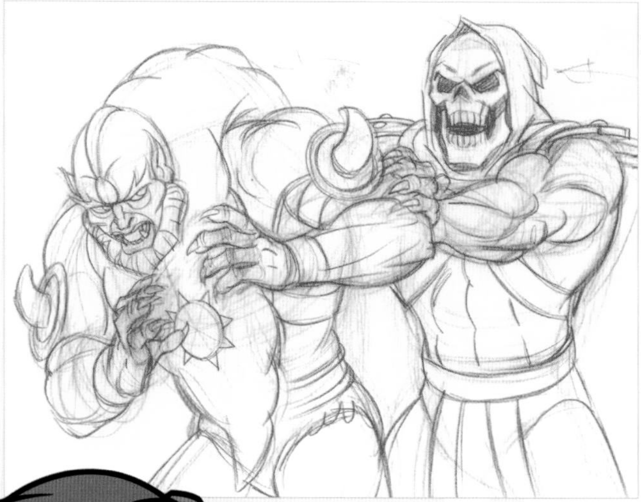

↑ Skeletor, seen here in pencil artwork from the cartoon, blames "Beastie" when plans go awry.

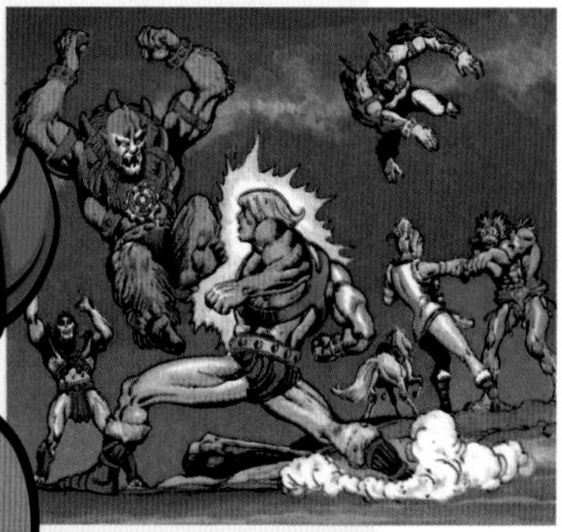

↑ Beast Man's ferocity in the minicomics was toned down for the animated series.

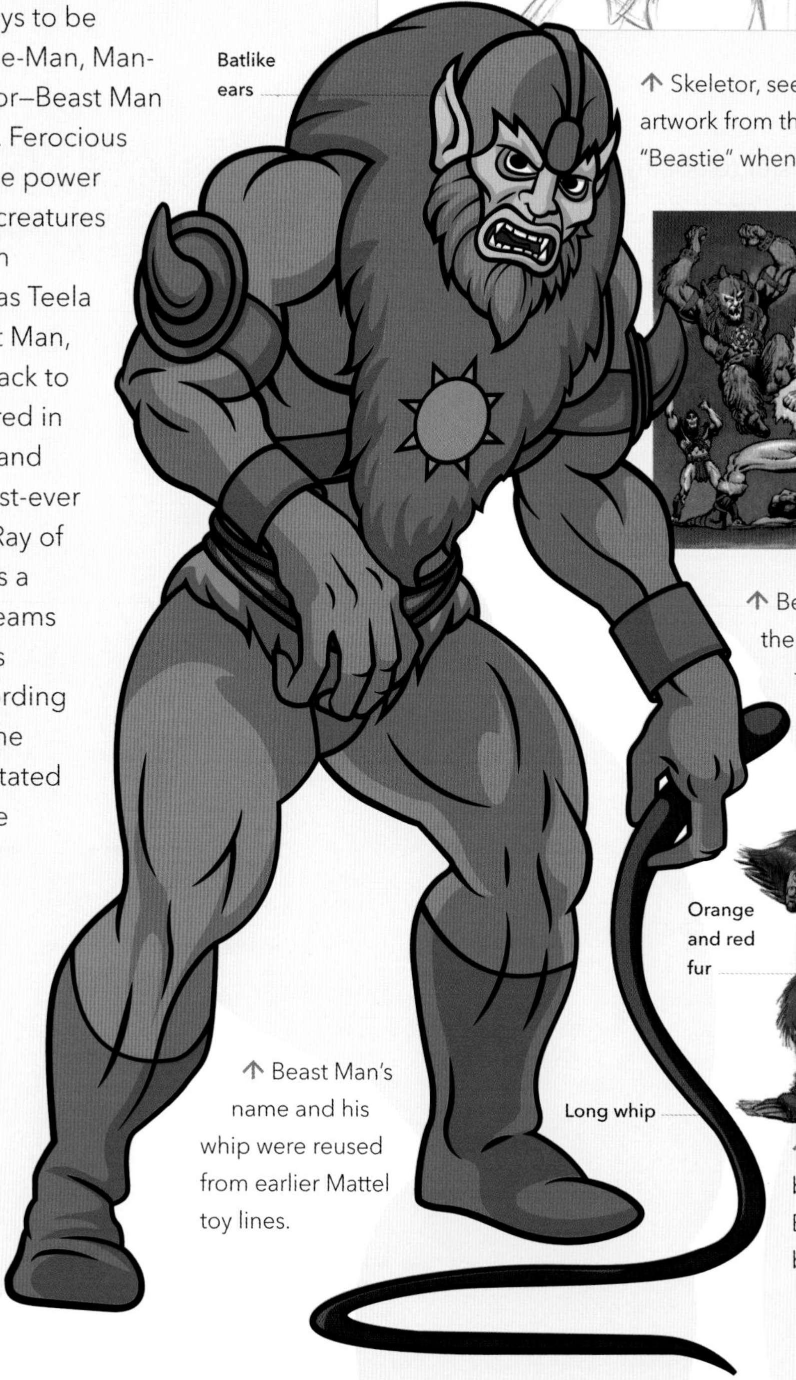
Batlike ears
Long whip

↑ Beast Man's name and his whip were reused from earlier Mattel toy lines.

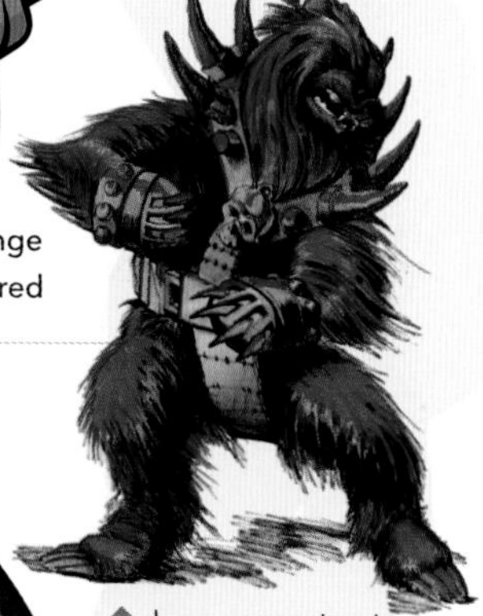
Orange and red fur

↑ In concept art by Mark Taylor, Beast Man had a bearlike look.

Mer-Man

Skeletor's most trusted henchman after Beast Man? You're looking at him: Mer-Man.

An ocean warlord and Skeletor's scaly servant, Mer-Man is an amphibious sea creature who possesses great strength on land and even greater powers underwater. He uses his powers of telepathy to control other sea creatures, taking great delight in making them attack the Heroic Warriors. Mer-Man first emerges from the depths in the original minicomics that accompany the action figures and then appears in a great number of episodes of the Filmation animated series, in which Alan Oppenheimer provides his distinctive gargling voice. Mer-Man sat out the 1987 feature film *Masters of the Universe*, but has reemerged in more recent iterations of the brand, in toys and animation.

RIVALRIES

Skeletor's two most powerful henchmen, Mer-Man and Beast Man, squabble among themselves for primacy with their master, throwing insults to one other: "Fuzzy-faced cretin," "fish-faced meathead!" Skeletor threatens to banish Mer-Man to a burning desert, where there's no water. Like all Skeletor's minions, he vows to one day overthrow Skeletor and rule alone!

→ Mer-Man's design was inspired by DC Comics' character Swamp Thing, as visualized in the 1970s by artist Bernie Wrightson.

Head fins

Sharp teeth

Yellow chest armor

↑ Mer-Man sometimes carries a sword or a trident.

Webbed feet

↑ Skeletor punishes Mer-Man for another bungled mission, in this minicomic panel.

MERMAN RAISES THE V.H.O.
BEAM FLARE FROM THE VHO & RAY GOES OS LFT

Trap Jaw

Evil and armed for combat, Trap Jaw is a cyborg with a deadly bite.

Concept art for Trap Jaw by Colin Bailey.

Laser weapon

Trap Jaw captures He-Man with his grabber attachment.

Leg armor

↑ Trap Jaw uses a huge range of weapons, including a laser gun, grabber, flamethrower, and freeze ray.

Trap Jaw is equipped with a range of deadly devices, including a mechanical chomping jaw filled with razor-sharp teeth and a robotic arm into which he can fit different weapons, such as a hook, a claw, and a rifle. He can even swing into action on a zip line, which threads through the loop on the top of his helmet.

ALIEN ORIGINS

One of the second wave of characters added to the toy line in 1983 after the first eight figures, Trap Jaw is a psychotic criminal from an alien dimension, according to the minicomic that accompanied his toy. His design somewhat resembles an action figure called Iron Jaw from Mattel's Big Jim toy line, who had a similar chomping jaw and a mechanical arm—with a touch of steel-toothed Jaws from the 1979 James Bond movie *Moonraker* thrown in. In the Filmation animated series, Trap Jaw is Skeletor's "wizard of weapons" and appears many times, often paired with Beast Man. He is one of the most bumbling of Skeletor's many incompetent warriors, easily confused and often complaining. Skeletor calls him a "tin-tongued dolt" and Teela describes him as a "lump of worthless ore"!

Tri-Klops

He's evil and sees everything: Tri-Klops uses his three different eyes to spy for Skeletor!

Skeletor's minion Tri-Klops wears a rotating visor helmet equipped with three mechanical eyes, each with a special type of vision. Designed by Mattel artist Roger Sweet, the toy, released in 1983, has a "daytime eye," which can see across long distances; a "nighttime eye," which sees in the dark; and an eye that sees around corners. In the minicomics, he could use all three eyes to see in different directions at once. In other media, he can see only out of the front eye and rotates his visor depending on which type of vision he requires. He could also use one eye to project bright light at enemies. In the Filmation animated series, Tri-Klops is less of a figure of fun than some of the Evil Warriors. Called the Hunter and operating as hired muscle, Skeletor employs Tri-Klops to defeat He-Man—he proves a near match for the "most powerful man in the universe" in strength.

VISUAL POWERS

In the animation, Tri-Klops's eyes are different shapes (square, circular, and triangular). The exact function of each eye varies, although they are usually: Distavision (the ability to see from far distances), Nightvision (the ability to see in the dark), and Gammavision (the ability to see through objects or around them). "Fire away, He-Man," he says, confidently. "I've seen every move long before you make it!"

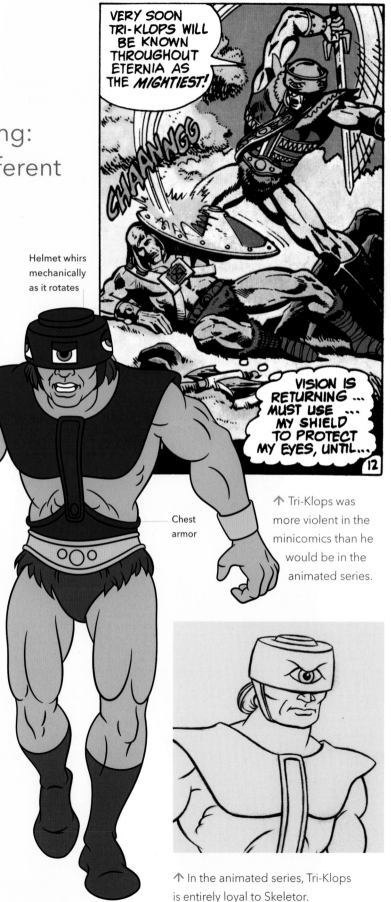

Helmet whirs mechanically as it rotates

VERY SOON TRI-KLOPS WILL BE KNOWN THROUGHOUT ETERNIA AS THE *MIGHTIEST*!

CHAANNGG

VISION IS RETURNING ... MUST USE ... MY SHIELD TO PROTECT MY EYES, UNTIL...

12

Chest armor

↑ Tri-Klops was more violent in the minicomics than he would be in the animated series.

↑ In the animated series, Tri-Klops is entirely loyal to Skeletor.

Minions and More

Skeletor's minions are a diverse gang of talented (and less-talented) individuals with strange powers, hybrid forms, and alien anatomies. Some, like Webstor and Clawful, prove cunning and occasionally reliable, almost worthy of Skeletor's respect—at least for a time—while others, such as Spikor, hardly know which way is up. In 1985, new arch-villain Hordak enters the toy line, bringing with him a new army of trouble-makers: adversaries to He-Man *and* Skeletor! Hordak is a sorcerer who uses magic and science. He is able to transform himself into machines of destruction, including a tank, a rocket, and a cannon. His legions of Horde Troopers would follow him right into Filmation's new animated series, *She-Ra: Princess of Power*.

SPIKOR

With a head and body covered in deadly spikes and a trident weapon for a hand, Spikor looks a formidable foe. However, in the animated series, he is dim-witted even by Evil Warrior standards. In some of his appearances in the show, his trident hand is missing.

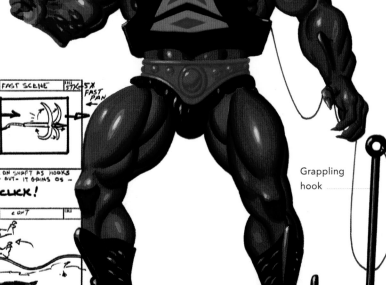

Multiple eyes on head

Laser rifle

Grappling hook

Webbed feet

WEBSTOR

In the animated series, this stealthy thief can fire a grappling hook on a rope from his backpack. He likes to scale the walls of the Royal Palace. He is also an "Evil Master of Escape" who can break out of any traps.

WEBSTOR
My grappler will stop you two....

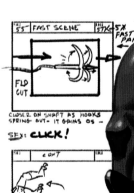

HE BENDS OVER - FIRES GRAPPLER
SHAFT LINE OS -

CLOSER ON SHAFT AS HOOKS
SPRING OUT - IT GAINS OS -

SFX: **CLICK!**

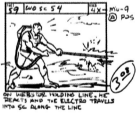

ON WEBSTOR HOLDING LINE, HE
REACTS AND THE ELECTRO TRAVELS
INTO SC ALONG THE LINE

AND GIVES HIM A BIG SHOCK.

WEBSTOR
YIIIII

WEBSTOR TUMBLES OS -

Bat shield

batlike ears

Bat emblem

Crossbow

HORDAK

TWO BAD

Samurai sword

JITSU

Scaly head

Gold chopping hand

Giant crushing claw

Mace

CLAWFUL

MODULOK

HORDAK

Before he was the main villain in *She-Ra: Princess of Power*, Hordak appeared in the Masters of the Universe toy line and animated series. He leads the Evil Horde, an army of savage warriors, and has a long-standing grudge against Skeletor.

TWO BAD

Two Bad is two evil beings in one: one creature is blue, the other is purple with scales and a prominent yellow monobrow. One of his heads often argues with the other.

JITSU

Jitsu is an Eternian master swordsman and martial artist who performs powerful karate chops with his super-sized golden right hand.

CLAWFUL

Half-man, half-lobster, Clawful has large claws instead of hands, one of which is often depicted as much larger than the other. In the animated series, his claws are the same size and he has fins like a sea creature.

MODULOK

A member of the Evil Horde, Modulok is a multibodied monster. In his minicomic, he mails a different part of his body to the Royal Palace, intending to piece himself together once inside. The animation simplified him, giving him a single body— and only one head.

The Snake Men

Slithering into the toy line in 1985, the Snake Men are a third faction of villains, in addition to the Evil Warriors and the Evil Horde. Kobra Khan had already appeared in the *He-Man and the Masters of the Universe* animated series, but the others were too late, since the show ceased production in 1985. Rattlor and Tung Lashor—in slightly adapted guises as members of the Evil Horde—appeared in the spin-off Filmation animated series, *She-Ra: Princess of Power*. Aligned to Skeletor, but not committed members of the Evil Warriors, the Snake Men challenge He-Man and the Heroic Warriors—while plotting their own conquest of Eternia in the name of their leader, King Hiss. In the distant past, the snake warriors formed a vast and powerful army until the Elders of Eternia banished them to a limbo underneath Snake Mountain. King Hiss plans for the reawakened Snake Men to be a mighty force again!

Decoy body

Snake body

KING HISS
The leader of the Snake Men, King Hiss tricks his foes by appearing to them as a heroic human. Then he sheds his human body casing to reveal his hideous form underneath: a mass of writhing serpents!

Snakes pop out

SNAKE FACE
Skeletor and King Hiss combine their powers to raise three ancient, buried towers on Eternia: from one, Snake Tower, Hiss manages to wake the most gruesome Snake Warrior of all—Snake Face, who can turn people to stone when they see his hideous snake-riddled face.

RATTLOR
Like Tung Lashor, whose sidekick he becomes, Rattlor is a Snake Soldier from another dimension. On the toy, his quick-strike neck shoots upward when a button is pressed on the back. He also has a battle rattle—produced by pieces of loose plastic inside his mold.

Neck telescopes upward

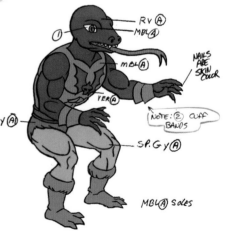

TUNG LASHOR
Skeletor and King Hiss brought Tung Lashor, seen here in an animation color drawing, back from another dimension. This Snake Soldier uses his extending tongue like a tentacle and a whip.

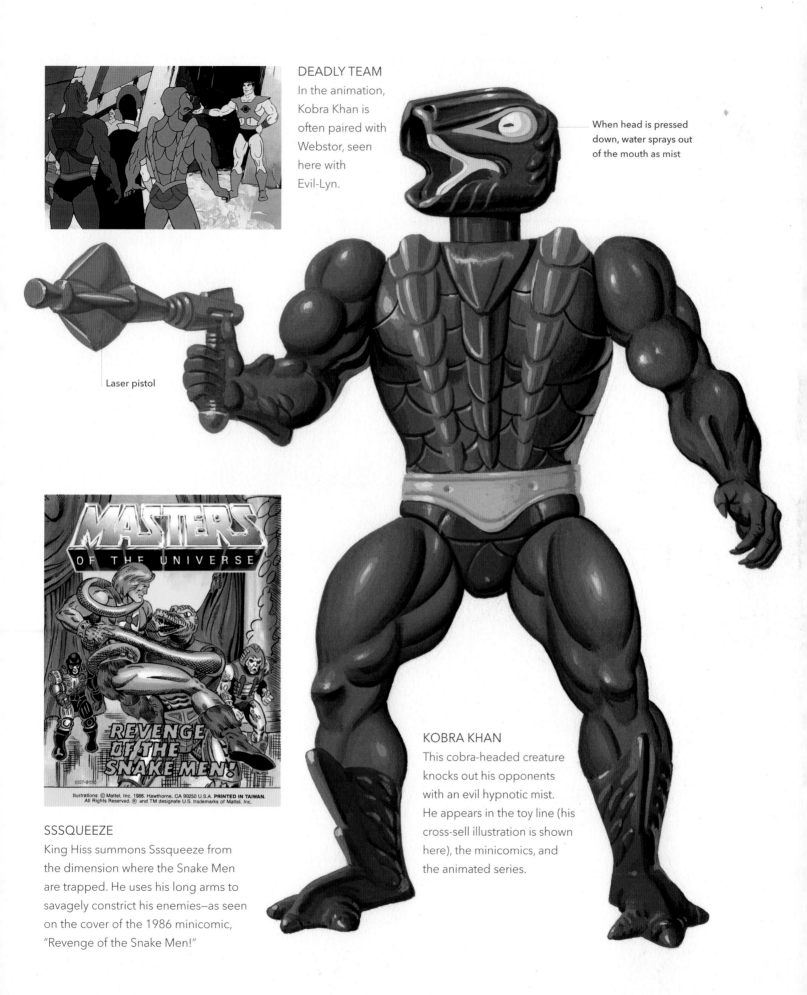

DEADLY TEAM

In the animation, Kobra Khan is often paired with Webstor, seen here with Evil-Lyn.

When head is pressed down, water sprays out of the mouth as mist

Laser pistol

SSSQUEEZE

King Hiss summons Sssqueeze from the dimension where the Snake Men are trapped. He uses his long arms to savagely constrict his enemies—as seen on the cover of the 1986 minicomic, "Revenge of the Snake Men!"

KOBRA KHAN

This cobra-headed creature knocks out his opponents with an evil hypnotic mist. He appears in the toy line (his cross-sell illustration is shown here), the minicomics, and the animated series.

MASTERS OF THE UNIVERSE

REVENGE OF THE SNAKE MEN!

0007-9130

Illustrations: © Mattel, Inc. 1986. Hawthorne, CA 90250 U.S.A. PRINTED IN TAIWAN.
All Rights Reserved. ® and TM designate U.S. trademarks of Mattel, Inc.

The Slime Pit

In 1976, Mattel introduced pots of green Slime into the toy aisle, creating an enduring hit toy with cool "yuck" factor. In 1986, Mattel added green Slime to the Masters of the Universe toy line with the Evil Horde's Slime Pit, creating a must-have toy for kids—though perhaps not for parents who had to clean the mess off the carpet! An action figure can be placed in the "Evil Pit of Gruesome Ooze" and held in place by a bony hand. When the dinosaur head is tilted forward, Slime oozes from the mouth, covering the unlucky figure in green gunk. The pit has its own minicomic, "Escape From the Slime Pit!"—and would go on to make an appearance in the *She-Ra: Princess of Power* animated series.

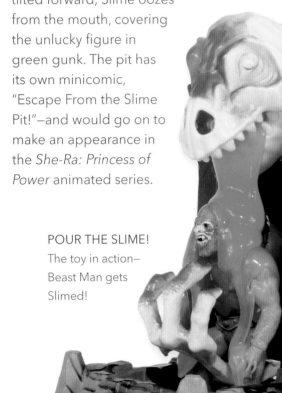

POUR THE SLIME!
The toy in action—Beast Man gets Slimed!

MAKING SLIME MONSTERS
In the minicomic, the Slime Pit transforms victims into mindless Slime monsters, who become Hordak's slaves.

"Horrible goop turns trapped warriors into Slime 'monsters!'"

Tagline from toy packaging

SLIME ACTION

The toy packaging features front-cover art by legendary painter William George, detailed action scenes on the back (shown below as original art), and Mattel's famous Slime logo.

64%

64%

48398

66%

Classic 1980s Collectibles

The massive success of *He-Man and the Masters of the Universe* took the brand to a new level: not only were sales of the toys going through the roof, kids could now find He-Man and Skeletor on every kind of product, from wallpaper and bed sets to stationery, duffle bags, and even record players—perfect for listening to your Masters of the Universe books-on-record. View-Master stereoscopic "3D" viewers had been around since the 1930s. The famous red version, introduced in the 1960s, was packaged in Masters of the Universe gift sets, with discs featuring art from the minicomics: the set shown here is a German/French edition with a viewer and three discs of art. Colorforms, a toy which dated back to the 1950s, offered MOTU characters on their trademark vinyl sheets, which stuck like magic to adventure scenes. Whether splashing in the bathtub with He-Man or Skeletor bubbles or packing your sandwiches in a He-Man lunch bag inside a Heroic Warriors metal lunch box, the 1980s was a golden era for the all-encompassing Masters of the Universe lifestyle!

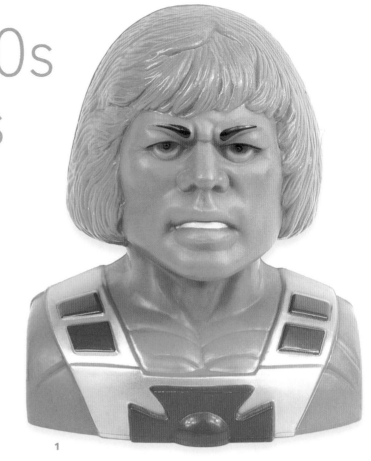

1

2

3

4

5

7

8

9

6

10

12

13

14

15

11

1 **Plastic He-Man coin bank,** HG Toys (1983)
2 **MOTU lunch box,** Aladdin Industries (1984)
3 **He-Man and Skeletor record player,** Power Tronic Works (1984)
4 **He-Man lunch bags,** Randim (1984)
5 **MOTU View-Master 3D gift set** (German/French edition),
   View-Master International Group (1983)
6 **MOTU bed set,** Burlington Industries (1983)
7 **Orku ink stamp,** HG Toys (1985)
8 **Skeletor keychain,** Spindex (1984)
9 **He-Man collectable eraser,** Spindex (1984)
10 **He-Man duffle bag,** Ero Leisure (1983)
11 **MOTU Colorforms Adventure Set,** Colorforms (1983)
12 **MOTU puffy stickers,** Gordy International (1982)
13 **He-Man bubble bath,** Mattel Inc. (1985)
14 **Power Sword and Power Shield set,** HG Toys (1985)
15 **MOTU Magic Slate,** Golden (1983)

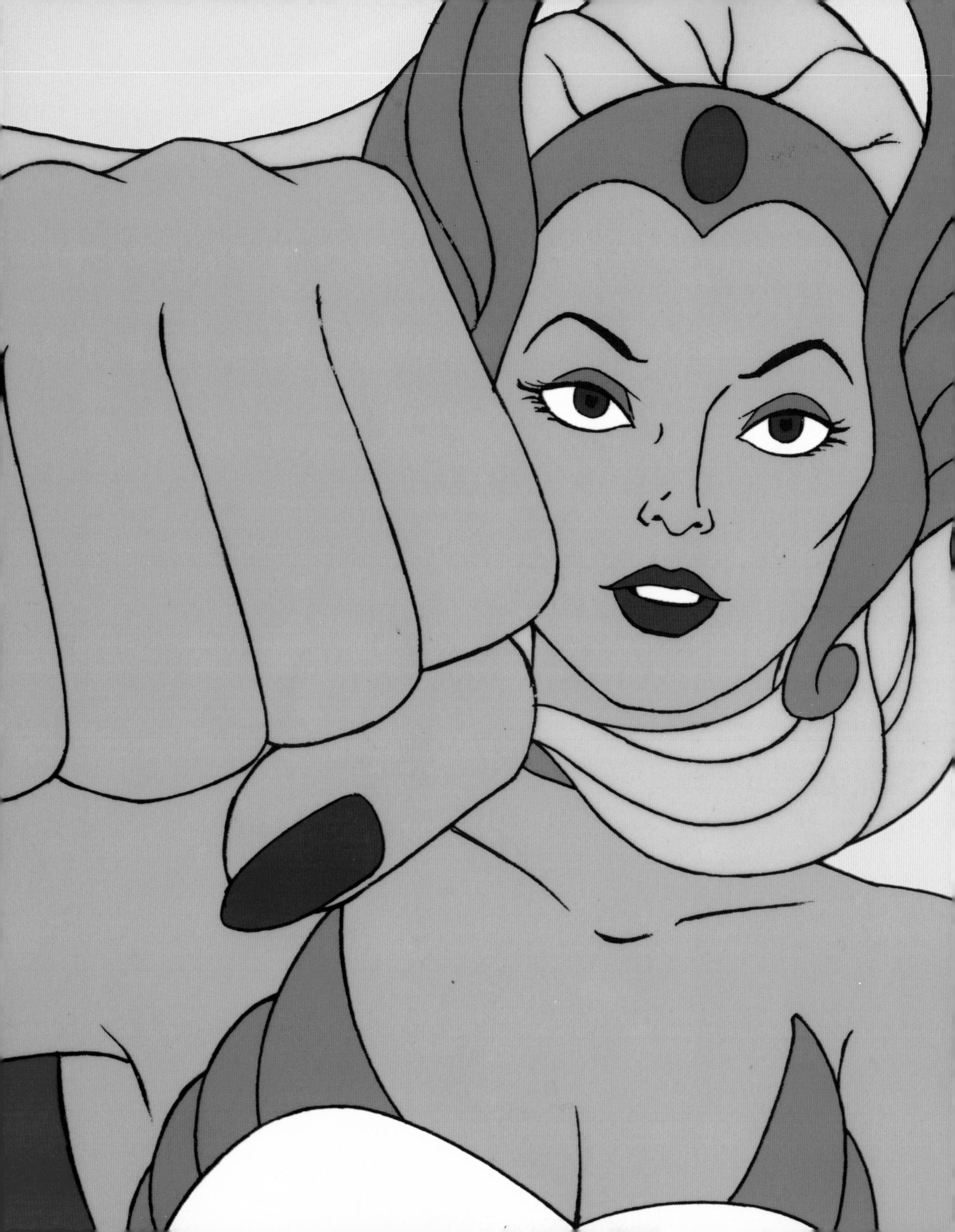

PRINCESS OF POWER

"For the honor of Grayskull … I am She-Ra!"

She-Ra

She-Ra, in a film cel from the animated series *(left)* and Horde Trooper toy *(below)*

The Dawn of a New Legend

A new hero, new villains, and a new TV show: the story of the leader of the Great Rebellion— She-Ra: Princess of Power.

↑ The poster for the *The Secret of the Sword* introduces She-Ra alongside He-Man, with "favorite characters from Master of the Universe" also promised. In the background, Castle Grayskull and Crystal Castle are visible.

When the phenomenal success of Masters of the Universe helped push sales of boys' toys at Mattel above those of girls' toys, including Barbie—traditionally the biggest part of Mattel's business—the company took note. Knowing that many girls already played with MOTU toys and enjoyed the cartoon, Mattel and Filmation decided to collaborate on a spin-off series aimed at a young female audience. Filmation writers Larry DiTillio and J. Michael Straczynski created an initial group of characters focused on He-Man's long-lost twin sister Adora, who transformed into She-Ra. Mattel and Filmation, working in close collaboration, introduced many more additional characters for the series, which debuted in 1985 and ran for two seasons—93 episodes—until 1986. To support the show's launch, Filmation edited the first five episodes from the show into a feature-length movie titled *He-Man and She-Ra: The Secret of the Sword.*

NEW WORLDS

The show takes place on the planet Etheria, brother planet to Eternia, which is controlled by Hordak and the Evil Horde. She-Ra and the Great Rebellion attempt to free their world from Hordak's clutches. Etheria has its version of Castle Grayskull—Crystal Castle, the secret source of magic on the planet, protected by a spirit keeper called Light Hope. He-Man and several of the characters from the Masters of the Universe animated series and toy line would continue to appear in the She-Ra television series, though Skeletor's role as master villain is largely replaced by Hordak.

↑ She-Ra reveals to Adam that she is his twin sister, in a layout sketch from the early episode "Reunions," which formed part of the feature film.

↑ The toy line for Princess of Power was heavily weighted toward She-Ra's army of rebels, with Catra the only villain in the first wave, followed by Entrapta the following year, as seen here on the back of the toy packaging.

↑ In this storyboard panel, the animators had not yet decided on the final form for Hordak. He would only be finalized by the final layout stage.

← The new series and toy line would introduce a new grouping of magical characters, including She-Ra, Sweet Bee, Peekablue, and their flying steeds.

She-Ra

The most powerful woman in the universe, She-Ra is the superhuman identity of Princess Adora.

← Adora is fiercely loyal to her cause: the liberation of her planet from the evil army she once served.

As a baby, Adora was kidnapped by Hordak, ruler of the planet Etheria and leader of an army known as the Evil Horde. A kindly Horde servant named Shakra raises Adora on Etheria, but Adora's good nature is diverted by an evil sorceress, Shadow Weaver, who puts a spell on her to make her selfish and ruthless. She becomes Force Captain Adora in the Evil Horde. Meanwhile, on Eternia, the Sorceress has a vision of a magical sword which she connects to Adora. She impels Prince Adam to travel to Etheria, where he discovers the truth: he has a long-lost twin sister. Adora is granted the Sword of Protection and gains the ability to transform into She-Ra. Princess Adora switches sides and joins the Great Rebellion that seeks to free Etheria from the Horde. The secret of Adora's transformation into She-Ra is known only by Prince Adam/He-Man, Cringer/Battle Cat, the Sorceress, Man-At-Arms, Orko, Spirit/Swift Wind, Light Hope, Madame Razz, Kowl, and Loo-Kee.

Winged headdress

→ She-Ra is strong-willed and forceful—she also knows the power of humor to disarm difficult situations.

"In the end, goodness will always win over evil."

She-Ra

Jewel of power

Sword of Protection

↑ She-Ra faces her former master, Hordak. The two are now sworn enemies.

↑ The design of She-Ra for the animated series went through many different versions.

↑ Much early concept art shows She-Ra with a winged crown.

SUPER POWERS

She-Ra is a powerful warrior with quick reflexes and superhuman strength. She communicates telepathically with her faithful winged unicorn mount, Swift Wind (who, when She-Ra is Adora, appears as an ordinary horse named Spirit). She-Ra's main weapon is the Sword of Protection, which she can command to transform into other things, including a shield, a chain, a rope, a ladder, and a blade of flame. The source of the Sword's power is a blue jewel embedded in its hilt, which can also project laserlike energy beams.

Prism stickers on crown

Cape made from shiny, irridescent fabric

Gold paint on boots

Removable wings (to transform back into Spirit)

Golden hooves

↑ The first She-Ra/Adora action figure featured a crown that could be turned upside down to form a mask.

↑ Called Swifty by She-Ra, Swift Wind can talk and communicate telepathically. He flies She-Ra into battle using his colorful wings.

Illustrations for a Princess of Power

She-Ra was initially developed as a female superhero counterpart to He-Man for the Masters of the Universe boys toy line—with a suitably rugged look. Once the decision was made to issue her in a new line of girls' toys, the concept was handed to the Girls Toy Design Group at Mattel, and the aesthetic was softened. Mattel's veteran doll designer and illustrator Noreen Porter created meticulously detailed illustrations of She-Ra, with more feminine proportions and superhero accessories. Jon Seisa, who worked at Mattel in the Girls' Toy Division in 1985, described Noreen Porter's illustrations as "highly technical, anatomically correct depictions. The sculptors could literally use her illustrations to sculpt directly from." Porter also worked on characters such as Spinerella and Catra, and a vehicle toy, the Bubble Carriage.

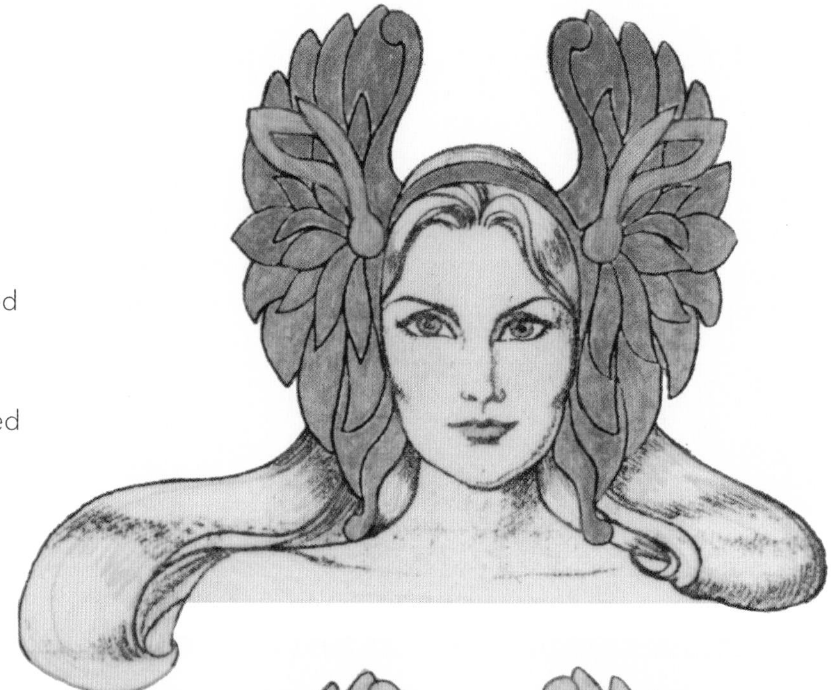

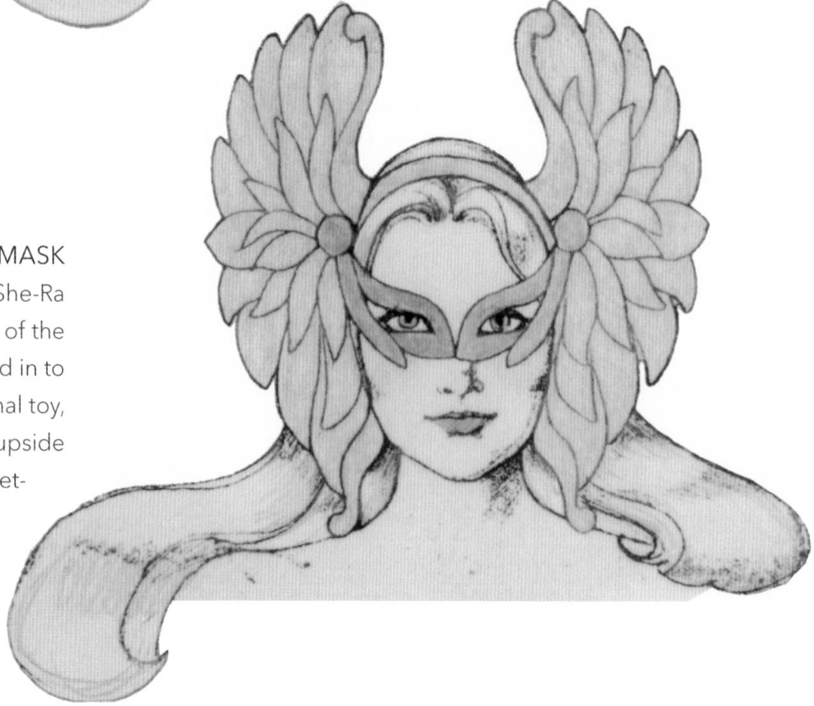

SUPERHERO MASK
Noreen Porter's color illustrations for She-Ra include a beautifully detailed rendition of the crown headdress, with wings that fold in to form a superhero-style mask. In the final toy, the crown can be turned completely upside down in order to transform to a helmet-mask. However, testing with kids showed that the headdress on top was much preferred over the mask.

ACTION OUTFIT

With the extraordinarily long hair, flowing cape, jeweled bodice, wrist gauntlets, and boots, many aspects of Noreen Porter's illustration match the final toy—the perfect combination of fashion icon and action hero!

Shield accessory

"[Noreen Porter's illustrations] were incredible masterpieces."

Jon Seisa, Former Art Director Of Advanced Concepts for the Girls' Toy Division at Mattel, 2012

Glimmer

Princess Glimmer is known as the "Guide who Lights the Way."

↑ In the animated series, Glimmer is the Princess of Bright Moon and one of the original founders of the Great Rebellion.

Princess Glimmer is one of the most powerful members of the Great Rebellion. Until Adora took command, teenage Glimmer was its leader. Now she acts as Adora's second-in-command, planning battle strategy and commanding the rebels when Adora is absent. Sometimes, her resentment at losing the leadership role comes out, causing tension with Adora. Glimmer is the daughter of Queen Angella and King Micah and Princess of one of Eternia's two satellites, the Bright Moon. Angella and Micah are the rightful rulers of Etheria, but since the takeover of their planet by the Evil Horde, the monarchical government rules in exile from Castle Brightmoon, also the current headquarters of the Great Rebellion. Angella rules alone while Micah has been captured by the Evil Horde.

LIGHT POWERS

Glimmer can manipulate light in many ways, from using it as a blinding weapon to firing beams that cut through solid objects. She can refract light to make herself and others invisible and even turn night into day for short periods. Princess Glimmer can also cast simple spells; teleport over short distances; and, when she is near her mother, fly without assistance. Glimmer is occasionally distracted by infatuations with handsome men—she is "[sighs] a big fan of Adam's …"

↑ → Queen Angella with feathered wings and her daughter Glimmer with her Staff of Light (and blonde hair), both shown in early character concept art.

← In Glimmer's toy, the staff and jeweled crown glow in the dark.

Staff of Light

← Seen in a pencil layout drawing for the animated series, Bow can cause chain reactions with a single shot: "Easy as bibble pie," as he would say.

Golden headband

← The breastplate on Bow's toy covers a heart feature: a button on the back makes it beat!

Bow

Bow is a "special friend who helps She-Ra"– but it is often She-Ra who helps him!

Though he has no magical powers, Bow is famed as a great archer–the best on all Etheria. His charisma and energy make him a popular and important member of the Great Rebellion and a great friend to Adora–possibly with romantic feelings for She-Ra. Bow loves the adulation of the rebels, which he encourages by performing magic tricks, playing the harp (his bow transforms into the musical instrument), and singing–though this is not always appreciated! Bow's best friend, Kowl, is one of his most outspoken critics: they share an old friendship but often spar with each other verbally, with Kowl usually winning the argument.

Red cape

← Bow is an athletic warrior who leaps into battle–sometimes without thinking. He uses his mastery of disguise to infiltrate the Evil Horde.

→ Concept art shows Bow with a quiver of arrows and a much larger bow than the final toy would have.

BOW IN BATTLE

From his home in Whispering Woods, Bow always seeks to help others, going into battle with his faithful horse Arrow. He is a brave and loyal warrior–but sometimes he needs She-Ra's help when the Horde captures him, often as a result of his own naiveté or impulsiveness.

Legendary Leaders

The members of the Great Rebellion come from near and far; from all corners of Etheria; from land, sea, and air; and even from off-world. Some are the rulers of realms. Queen Frosta leads the Snow People in the Kingdom of Snows, located high in the Dreaming Mountains. Princess Mermista's underwater kingdom, Salineas, is protected by the Pearl of Power, which gives her people control over the waters and sea creatures—they are drawn into the war when the Horde tries to steal the pearl. Castaspella is a Sorceress-Queen who rules the enchanted Kingdom Of Mystacor, an Etherian land where castles float in midair. Others have humble origins. Flutterina was a servant girl, but her powers allow her to control butterflies of all kinds. Sweet Bee helps guide her people, the Andreenids, or Bee People, to a new home on Etheria. All are legendary leaders!

Comb

Yellow shield

SWEET BEE
Sweet Bee is a daring scout for the Bee People, who join the Rebellion against the Evil Horde. In the animated series, she can fly and craft objects from honeycomb; her toy features glow-in-the-dark antennae and wings.

FLUTTERINA
Flutterina is an airborne fighter who can repel enemies when she beats her large wings. She controls butterflies and uses them as spies and messengers—and can even completely transform herself into a butterfly to escape capture.

PRINCESS of POWER

A MOST UNPLEASANT PRESENT

HAS GLOVES

TU-(1A)
SFK-(1)
BL-(A)
BL-(A)
(1)
(1)
BL-(A)
TU-(1A)
(1)
BL-(A)
TU-(1)
(1)
SOLES (5) — **NOTE**

FROSTA

Shown in an animation color guide, Queen Frosta is a powerful ice sorceress who rules the Kingdom of Snows on Etheria from Castle Chill. She can control ice and snow.

Distinctive red hair

Lightning bolt emblem

Magic hypnosis wheel

Wheel spins to "enchant" enemies

Lightning bolt design on boots

Water sprays from jewel

Shiny silver tail dress

Shell backpack can be filled with water

MERMISTA

Mermista is the Princess of Salineas, an underwater city on Etheria. She can control the element of water and communicate with sea creatures. Mermista defies her father, King Mercia, by joining the Rebellion; he wishes to stay out of the battle with the Horde.

CASTASPELLA

Castaspella—shown here as a toy and in concept artwork—is a powerful sorceress who rules the Mystacor Kingdom on Etheria. She trained alongside Shadow Weaver—they are now enemies. Her spells include hypnotism and stun blasts.

Able Allies

Some of the amazing members of the Great Rebellion come from humble backgrounds, and, through strange twists of fate, are magically transformed into powerful beings who use their superhuman powers to help the cause. Flutterina was a poor serving girl known as "Small One," who was enslaved in a grim castle. She-Ra rescues her and takes her to the Crystal Castle, where Light Hope magically envelops her in a cocoon, from which she emerges as Flutterina. Netossa has no magical abilities at all, but proves that well-practiced skill and quick-thinking can overcome much physically stronger foes. Peekablue also proves that being a physical fighter isn't everything: her powers of sight prove crucial to the Rebellion.

Pink and red styling used on concept art

Trick "evil" face

Comb

Blooming flower backpack

Mirror held in concept art

Long ponytail

PERFUMA
Scent-sational Perfuma can control plants and use their scent to put her enemies to sleep. Her toy features a backpack that blooms into a flower when a slider is pushed; it can be used as a hand-held, scent-blasting weapon.

DOUBLE TROUBLE
Double Trouble works as a spy. She can transform her facial features, tricking enemies such as Catra into trusting her so she can learn their secret plans. The face of her toy can switch from good to evil using a dial on the back.

Feathers open like a fan

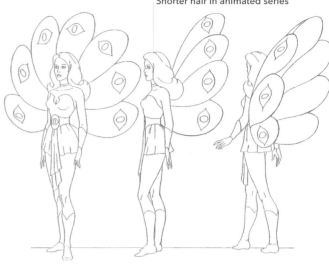

Shorter hair in animated series

PEEKABLUE

Shy scout Peekablue has peacocklike feathers which, when spread out, allow her enhanced sight: she can peer across vast distances, even into other worlds, and "see" things before they happen.

NETOSSA

Instead of using magical powers, Netossa has taught herself the ability to surprise her enemies by swiftly tossing her net over them. She pulls the drawstrings to capture them completely.

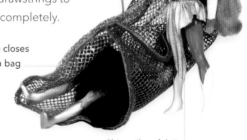

Cape closes into a bag

Net cape, seen in turnaround sketch for animated series

Shiny silver fabric

SPINNERELLA

Spinnerella, seen here with Netossa, can spin at great speeds, creating a whirlwind that can clear a path before her. Her toy slots into a scooter device to make it spin.

Spinning scooter can also be worn as backpack

Turnaround sketch for animated series

Rebel Supporters

Supporters of the Great Rebellion come in all shapes and sizes!

Many Etherians wish to assist the Great Rebellion to defeat Hordak and the Evil Horde once and for all. Madame Razz is a witch who lives in the vast enchanted forest known as the Whispering Woods—also home to the Rebel encampment. She tries to use her ability to brew potions and cast spells to help, but, more often than not, she forgets or mispronounces the spell—even so, she gets results ... somehow! In this, she is similar to Orko, who she befriends when they meet. Madame Razz is one of the four people on Etheria who know that Adora is She-Ra. Through Adora, she also learns the secret of Prince Adam being He-Man. Broom is Madame Razz's flying best friend; he provides transport for Madame Razz (and, sometimes, She-Ra).

WITTY SCOUT

Kowl is one of a near-extinct race called the Kolians. Though timid, he often flies above the rebel camp in the Whispering Woods to look for signs of attack or other dangers. He bickers with Bow, using his wit, intelligence, and sharp tongue to win the argument. He is one of the few who know that Adora and She-Ra are one and the same.

HIDES AND "SEES"!

Loo-Kee is a small creature called a Kon-Seal. He follows She-Ra and the other Rebels, hiding behind trees, bushes, and elsewhere. At the end of almost every episode, Loo-Kee emerges and asks the viewers if they saw where he was hiding. He then reveals his hiding place to the viewers and tells the moral of the story. Loo-Kee knows the dual identities of Adora/She-Ra and Adam/He-Man—though this is not mentioned in either show's opening credits.

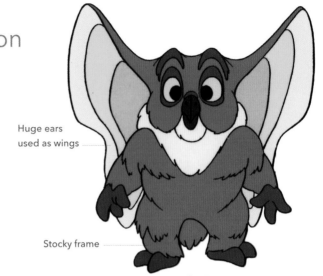

Huge ears used as wings

Stocky frame

KOWL

↑ Although Kowl's race is almost extinct, other members exist, including Kowla, with whom he is romantically ... tied—as seen in this pencil layout.

Eyes move as toy moves

Blue tail

LOO-KEE

← "Size is not the true measure of one's worth," says Loo-Kee. "Little people, like you and me, can do big things."

SEE REVISED LAYOUT

(EFX OKAY)

↑ Madame Razz casts a spell, in a pencil layout sketch from the animated series.

Tufts of hair spouting from hole in hat

Crooked hat

← Like Orko, Madame Razz's face is mostly obscured by her hat.

↑ Madame Razz, Broom, and Kowl must work together to rescue the Rebels from a sleeping spell cast by Shadow Weaver disguised as a young magician, in the episode "Three Courageous Hearts."

MADAME RAZZ

Crystal Castle

Standing at the top of Skydancer Mountain, the Crystal Castle is the most magical place on Etheria. Protected and kept secret by a spirit called Light Hope, it contains secrets from the time of the First Ones—the founders of Etheria. This mysterious fortress serves as a refuge and place of power for She-Ra. In 1985, Crystal Castle became the first play set in the Princess of Power toy line, described on its packaging as a "Shimmering castle of fantasy and fun for She-Ra and her friends."

HOME OF SHE-RA
The table in the toy set comes with a map of Etheria as a printed sticker on the top.

GOLDEN EXTERIOR
The cloud decoration on the exterior links to the animated series, in which the castle is located above the clouds.

Secret entrance

Clothes stand

Throne moves up and down as an elevator

Main entrance

Treasure chest with hidden storage for accessories

Furry purple rug

Canopy bed

INSIDE THE CASTLE
The interior of the set include a throne that operates as an elevator, a canopy bed with a sponge mattress, and a table with a map of Etheria on it.

ROCKY CASTLE
In this concept artwork from 1984, the play set is designed with a rugged, mountainous exterior and a sparkling, Aladdin's Cave-style interior setting.

Jeweled throne

Lantern bedpost

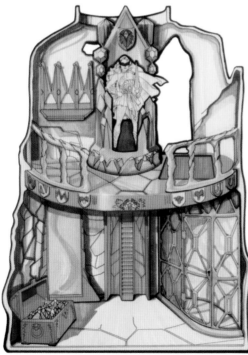

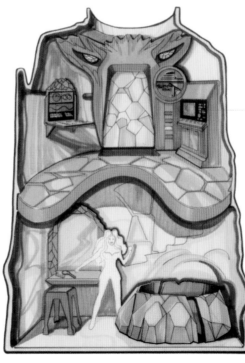

Computer console

HIGH-TECH CASTLE
This conceptualization, also from 1984, has some of the features of the final play set, such as the throne-elevator. The high-tech computer stations on the second floor were ultimately not incorporated.

Magical Transport

The members of the Great Rebellion travel by a variety of magical means. She-Ra has her pink unicorn, Swift Wind, and Bow has the heroic Arrow, a flying (usually) blue horse—just watch out for evil Catra flying the other way on her mischievous horse, Storm. When the rebels need to leave the Whispering Woods in a hurry, they clamber onboard Enchanta, a giant swan that flies at breathtaking speeds, twisting and turning with exceptional maneuverability. On water, they travel by Sea Harp, a musical seahorse boat. Most mysterious is Butterflyer, a living flying vehicle who She-Ra coaxed out of a long slumber and befriended.

Mane can be styled in different ways

Wings slot into notches in the body

Golden hooves

HEROIC STEED

The "true blue" toy version of Arrow "flies Bow to victory" and includes a comb to groom the horse's mane and tail. In the animated series, Arrow is one of the fastest steeds on Etheria.

She-Ra leaped between Butterflyer's wings and beckoned her friends to join her. "Quick, everyone! We must help Perfuma stop Catra from ruining the beautiful gardens!" She-Ra said. In an instant they were airborne, headed for the Laughing Swan Inn.

Delicate wings

Figures sit inside

Butterfly held in hands

WINGED FLYER

The rebels nestle between Butterflyer's wings to go on magical flights. Butterflyer appears in the cartoon and the minicomics (*left*). The toy (*above*) works as a carrying case for up to eight figures.

UNPRODUCED TOYS

The Flutter Plane, seen here in concept artwork (*right*), appeared in the animated series and minicomics but was not made into a toy. The two-seater winged vehicle (*below*) may have been an early conceptualization for the Butterflyer.

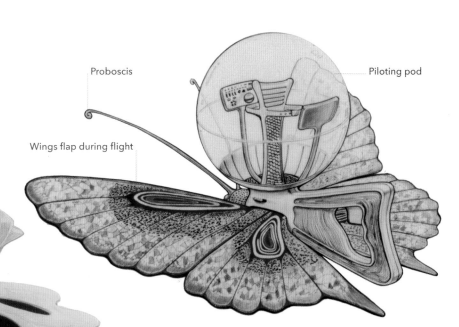

Proboscis

Piloting pod

Wings flap during flight

She-Ra holding the reins

Wings (and tail) slot into notches on the body

Fluffy pink mane

Musical "harp" feature contained within seat

SWAN FLYER

A friend of the Rebellion, Enchanta can carry four passengers on her back. Being a swan, she likes to spend time with Mermista at the Crystal Falls.

MUSICAL SEAHORSE

The rebels traveled across water in the Sea Harp, a blue-and-pink seahorse-headed boat with reins for a pilot to steer. The rear seat of the toy accommodates two figures and features a musical harp—"played" by moving a slider from side to side.

Hordak

The ruthless leader of the Evil Horde is the most evil being in the universe.

Leader of the Evil Horde and ruler of Etheria from his lair in the Fright Zone, Hordak is a vampiric being with sharp teeth and pointed, batlike ears. He uses dark magic but prefers technology. "Bah! I should never rely on sorcery," he snorts in the 1985 episode, "A Loss for Words." "That's what I hated about Skeletor! Science, machinery ... [snorts] ... these I can count on!" Hordak can transform his body into machines, including an energy cannon and a tank. This horrid fiend was once Skeletor's mentor and was responsible for kidnapping Adora when she was an infant. But Skeletor betrayed Hordak, who escaped to the planet Etheria with Adora. As Adora grew up, Hordak was careful to hide his cruel side from her, but, with the help of Shadow Weaver's spells, he brainwashed Adora into taking a senior role in the Evil Horde. When Adora defected to the Great Rebellion, Hordak became her arch nemesis.

EVIL ORIGINS

Although Hordak is the primary villain in the animated series *She-Ra: Princess of Power*, his action figure first appeared in 1985 as part of the Masters of the Universe line, where he was an enemy of He-Man *and* Skeletor. His toy was packaged with the minicomic "Hordak: The Ruthless Leader's Revenge!", in which Hordak tricks Skeletor into forming an alliance with him, then betrays him by capturing Snake Mountain for himself. Hordak's henchmen also frequently betray him and side with Skeletor. Hordak's only truly reliable ally is a small creature named Imp: "The only one around here I can trust," reckons Hordak.

↑ In the minicomic "Hordak: The Ruthless Leader's Revenge!", the evil leader wears a gray uniform. In the animated series, it becomes a less-stark blue color.

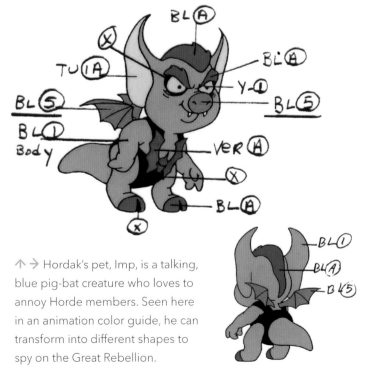

↑ → Hordak's pet, Imp, is a talking, blue pig-bat creature who loves to annoy Horde members. Seen here in an animation color guide, he can transform into different shapes to spy on the Great Rebellion.

• THIN BLACK LIPS

• 6½ ft. TALL
• WHITE FACE
• BLACK ARMOR, LOIN FUR & BOOTS
• TRASFORMATION BODY

HORDAK

↑ Hordak went through many different concepts until the final masklike design was settled on. Mattel artist and toy designer Roger Sweet said it was modeled on traditional African masks.

← Horde Prime is the only being with authority over Hordak. According to Hordak, he is "ruler of a thousand worlds, the most feared being ... [snorts] ... in three galaxies."

→ Hordak has a cyborg-like face with piercing red eyes. He wears a bone collar and armor emblazoned with the Horde bat symbol.

"[snorts] No more Mr. Robo-Nice Guy!"

Hordak, "Hordak's Power Play," 1987

Shadow Weaver

This foul fiend is the evil mistress of advanced sorcery.

A powerful sorceress, Shadow Weaver is Hordak's second-in-command. Swathed in a long gown with a headdress and veil covering most of her face, she was once an apprentice to a great wizard named Norwyn in the kingdom of Mystacor on Etheria. However, when Hordak invaded the planet, she betrayed Norwyn—and her own people—and assisted the Horde in return for greater powers, which left her face and her personality disfigured. She renamed herself Shadow Weaver and became Norwyn's mortal enemy. When Hordak kidnapped Princess Adora when she was an infant, it was Shadow Weaver who cast a spell on her so that she would believe the deceptions of the Horde and blindly follow their evil ways.

DARK POWERS

Shadow Weaver uses her nearly limitless magical powers to cast "shadow magic"—used to trap people. She can also control people's minds, throw blasts of energy, disguise herself, and teleport to other planets. She plots with Hordak at his base of operations in a dark, polluted landscape called the Fright Zone, but she lives in Horror Hall: a terrifying structure at the top of a volcano guarded by a two-headed dragon named Nightfire. Several Horde Troopers are posted here as guards and Shadow Weaver is also attended by her familiar, a vulture called Styrax, who carries messages to Hordak. Created by Filmation for the animated series, Shadow Weaver did not have a figure in the original Princess of Power toy line, though she appeared in the Masters of the Universe Classics toy line in 2012.

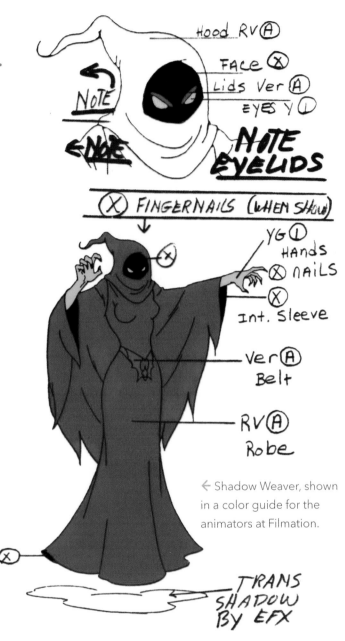

← Shadow Weaver, shown in a color guide for the animators at Filmation.

"Oh, Shadow Weaver, you are so clever."

Shadow Weaver, "Something Old, Something New," 1986

← In a pencil layout sketch for the animated series, Shadow Weaver guards the Sword of Protection before Adora gains possession of it in the gripping early sequence of episodes.

↑ Shadow Weaver's powers are at their strongest within the walls of her lair, Horror Hall.

→ Once young and beautiful, Shadow Weaver became greatly altered by her conversion to evil. She allows only her yellow eyes and green hands and arms to be seen under her robe.

Catra

Cunning, catlike villain Catra has her claws out for She-Ra.

Hair hasn't become the long mane she eventually acquires

Catra wears a magical mask that, when pulled over her eyes, gives her immense powers and the ability to transform into a fierce panther. Born on the island of Purrsia, she witnessed the arrival of the Evil Horde but chose to help it to enslave Purrsia, betraying her own people. Witnessing her malign abilities, Hordak made her a Horde member. Hordak gave her magical mask, which he had stolen from the Queen of the Magicats, from which all her power derived. In addition to shape-shifting powers, the mask enables Catra to teleport and to fire beams at her opponents. In the minicomics and the toy line, Catra has a foul-tempered flying horse named Storm and, seen also in the animation, a pet lion named Clawdeen.

UNTRUSTWORTHY DEPUTY

Initially, Catra was going to be the main villain in the Princess of Power toy line. However, when the Evil Horde were brought into the Filmation animated series, she becomes Hordak's Force Captain—a position that had been Adora's until she defected to the Great Rebellion. Catra leads a squad typically composed of Grizzlor, Leech, Mantenna, and Scorpia. However, Catra's loyalty to Hordak is only to make herself more powerful—she secretly plans to overthrow him, even teaming up with Skeletor to do so. Catra appears in most of the minicomics, where she operates both on her own and aligned with the Horde. She is seen to harbor an extreme jealousy of She-Ra, persecuting her and craving anything that she has—including Bow's affection.

↑ In this concept illustration, Catra carries a lion mask, which would become a shield in the final toy. The bodice detailing is close to final and she wears gloves instead of gauntlets, as does her toy; her tail has not yet been added.

↑ In the miniciomics, Catra is a witch who plots against She-Ra to rule Etheria. When she wears her cat mask, she can transform into a fierce black cat.

Cat mask

Saddle

→ In the animated series, Catra shows great intelligence and cunning. She plots against She-Ra and the Great Rebellion—and against her own side, too.

↑ With curly pink hair, pink flocking, and jewel eyes, Clawdeen carries Catra to many adventures and apparently also taught her the skill of transforming into a cat.

↑ Catra's toy transforms into a cat with the simple action of putting on her cat mask. Her spring-back "action waist" also gives her a scratching feature.

The Evil Horde

Reporting only to Horde Prime, Hordak is the leader of the Evil Horde, with Shadow Weaver as his second-in-command and Catra operating as Force Captain. Horde Troopers serve as the Horde's invasion and occupation army. Horde Trooper variants, including Jet Troopers and Naval troopers, provide specialized support. The Horde recruits allies and enforcers from conquered worlds—those who crave power often realize that joining the Horde is the best way to further it. Horde technicians use twisted science to create grotesque minions and henchmen to do their bidding, such as Mantenna, with his extendible eyes that pop out on stalks, and the truly loathsome Leech.

TRICKY VILLAIN
Operating as Catra's assistant and the Horde's technician, Entrapta, seen in the animation (left) and her toy (right), invents traps and machines. She also uses her incredibly long hair braids to entrap her enemies.

Long hair can be twisted and styled

Silver-painted legs

Sharp teeth

Horde bat emblem

Red crossbow

Suction-cup hand

VILE SUCKER
Amphibianlike Leech sucks and drains the life-force from his opponents, using his sucker mouth and hands. Just the sight of him licking his foul lips is enough to terrorize Etherian villagers.

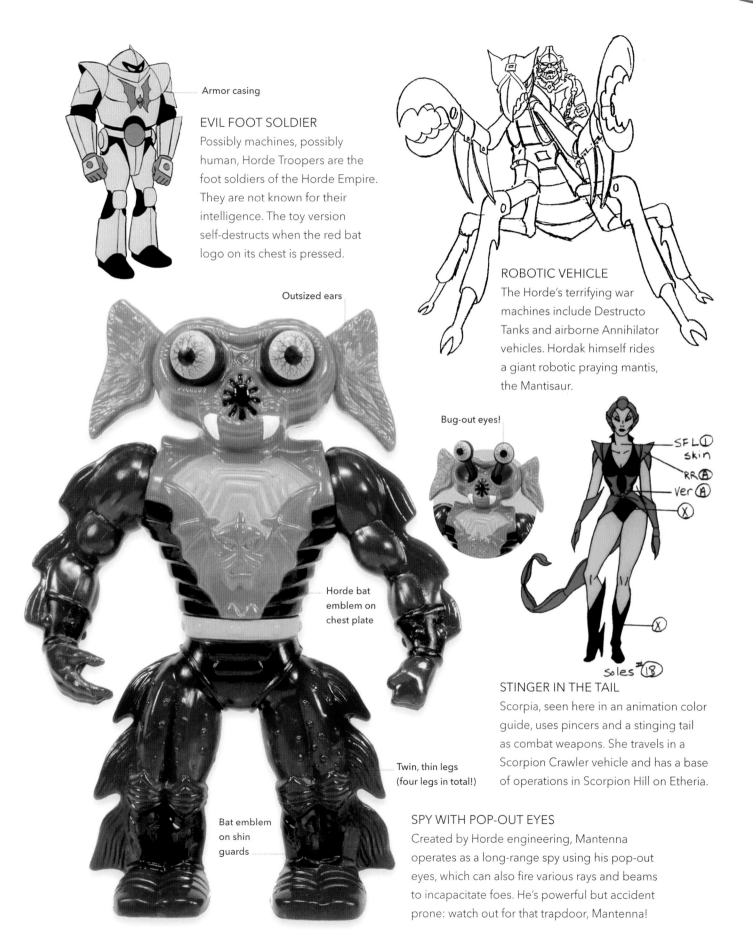

Armor casing

EVIL FOOT SOLDIER

Possibly machines, possibly human, Horde Troopers are the foot soldiers of the Horde Empire. They are not known for their intelligence. The toy version self-destructs when the red bat logo on its chest is pressed.

Outsized ears

ROBOTIC VEHICLE

The Horde's terrifying war machines include Destructo Tanks and airborne Annihilator vehicles. Hordak himself rides a giant robotic praying mantis, the Mantisaur.

Bug-out eyes!

Horde bat emblem on chest plate

SFL① skin
RR Ⓐ
Ver Ⓐ
Ⓧ

Ⓧ

Soles #18

STINGER IN THE TAIL

Scorpia, seen here in an animation color guide, uses pincers and a stinging tail as combat weapons. She travels in a Scorpion Crawler vehicle and has a base of operations in Scorpion Hill on Etheria.

Twin, thin legs (four legs in total!)

Bat emblem on shin guards

SPY WITH POP-OUT EYES

Created by Horde engineering, Mantenna operates as a long-range spy using his pop-out eyes, which can also fire various rays and beams to incapacitate foes. He's powerful but accident prone: watch out for that trapdoor, Mantenna!

The Fright Zone

The Fright Zone is the dismal location where Hordak and the Evil Horde set up their horrible base of operations. From here, Hordak plans his schemes, houses his weapons, trains his army, and reprimands his henchmen. The toy line and *She-Ra: Princess of Power* animated series pictured it quite differently. In the toy line and the minicomics, it is a place of crumbling rocks and blasted trees, filled with traps and a dungeon. This version was never seen in the *He-Man and the Masters of the Universe* animated series. In the She-Ra animation, the Fright Zone is an industrial hinterland, from which Hordak's towers and factories emerge.

> "The Fright Zone. Now the fun begins!"
>
> She-Ra, "The Caregiver," 1986

HORDE FACTORIES

In the *She-Ra: Princess of Power* animated series, the Fright Zone is depicted as a bleak, polluted landscape where large factories belch out smoke, as seen in these detailed storyboard panels for the episode "Into Etheria" from 1985.

ORIGINAL FRIGHT ZONE

In the minicomic "Grizzlor: The Legend Comes Alive!", Hordak stands before a rock tower, a dead tree, and a dungeon door, which resemble the play set version of the Fright Zone.

STRONGHOLD OF TERROR

As depicted in William George's art for the play set box, the Fright Zone lurks beneath dramatic red skies, with a serpent-infested cave and an eerily glowing dungeon.

Princess of Power Memorabilia

The range of merchandise for *She Ra: Princess of Power* was smaller than that for Masters of the Universe, but it still extended the brand and its colorful characters into a great many categories, including stationery, books, bedding, and dress-up. She-Ra herself appears on the widest variety of items, from bubble bath and stickers to digital watches (with a smart yellow strap and five—yes, five!—functions) and more. However, some products feature larger groupings of the lead characters: the lunch box shown here has a line-up of Peekablue, Glimmer, Angelica, Castapella, She-Ra, Frosta, Catra (boo, hiss!), and Flutterina. For anyone wanting to live out the fantasy, costume and mask sets from Ben Cooper provided a plastic mask and two-piece costume (a dress and cape). The same manufacturer also made a dress-up costume for Hordak, which was branded Masters of the Universe.

1

2

3

5

4

7

6

8

1 **Princess of Power lunch box,** Aladdin Industries (1985)
2 **She-Ra sticker valentines,** Hallmark (1985)
3 **She-Ra bubble bath,** DuCair Bioessences (1985)
4 **She-Ra and Swift Wind TV tray** (1985)
5 **She-Ra costume and mask,** Ben Cooper (1985)
6 **Surprise in Whispering Woods book and cassette tape,** Kid Stuff (1986)
7 **She-Ra digital watch,** Nelsonic Industries (1985)
8 **She-Ra party hats,** Unique Industries (1985)

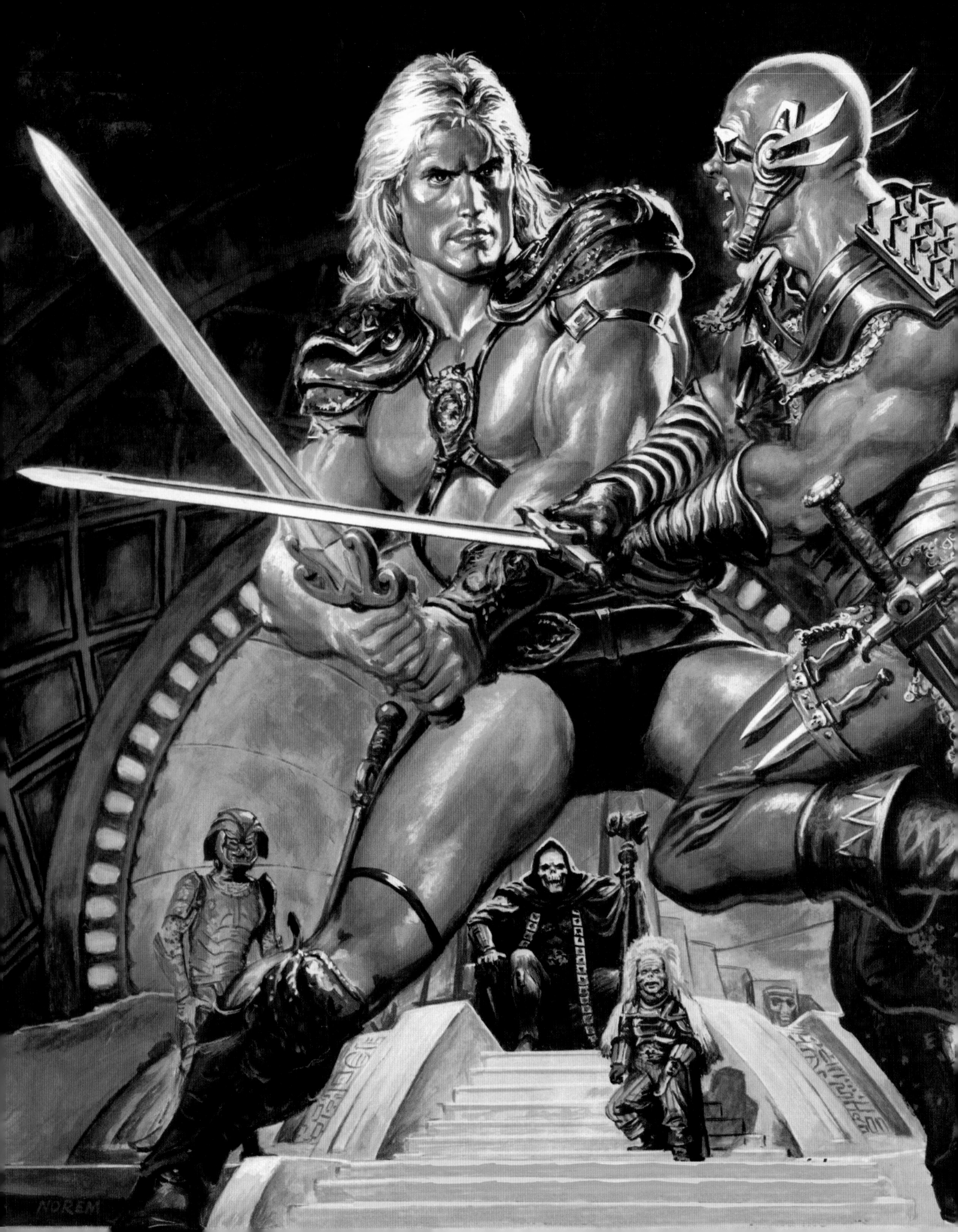
NOREM

THE MOTION PICTURE

"Let this be
our final battle!"

Skeletor to He-Man,
*Masters of the Universe:
The Motion Picture*, 1987

A 1987 magazine poster illustration by
Earl Norem *(left)* and Ralph McQuarrie
poster concept sketch *(below)*

Masters of the Universe

In 1987, He-Man leapt onto the big screen in a live-action feature film entitled *Masters of the Universe*.

In the movie, He-Man is played by Swedish actor Dolph Lundgren, fresh from his breakout role in *Rocky IV* in 1985. He faces arch nemesis Skeletor, brilliantly interpreted by Frank Langella, who threw himself into the role partly as a result of seeing how much his then-4-year-old son loved He-Man (and Skeletor) toys. Skeletor has conquered Eternia and rules from Castle Grayskull, forcing He-Man, Man-At-Arms, and Teela to seek entry to the castle using a Cosmic Key provided by a dwarflike being named Gwildor. However, the key also has the ability to transport its holder to any place throughout space and time, and He-Man and friends end up on Earth, quickly followed by Skeletor, Evil-Lyn, and their army. Teaming up with two Earth teenagers named Kevin and Julie, He-Man and the Masters return to Eternia to save the Universe. At the climax, they battle Skeletor at the top of Castle Grayskull, assisted by Evil-Lyn, who turns against her master. Skeletor is stripped of his powers and crashes into a vast pit. However, in a postcredits scene, Skeletor is seen at the bottom of the pit, vowing, "I'll be back!"

PLANS FOR A SEQUEL

A sequel to the movie was begun, though it was abandoned. Provisionally entitled *Masters of the Universe 2: Cyborg*, it was to have been set on a postapocalyptic Earth (Skeletor's doing, of course) and would have featured Trap Jaw and She-Ra. Some of the sets and costumes had already been created and were ultimately used in the 1989 movie *Cyborg*, starring Jean-Claude Van Damme.

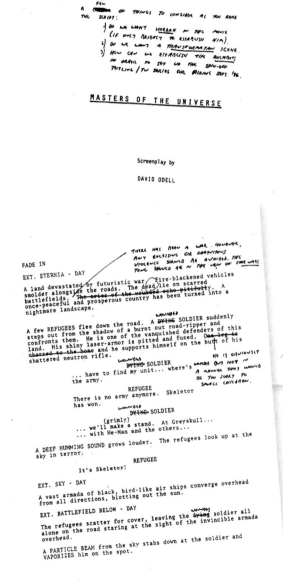

↑ The script was written by David Odell, a co-writer on *The Muppet Show* who also wrote the screenplay for Jim Henson and Frank Oz's *The Dark Crystal* (1982). Corrections show hints of violence being toned down for a young audience.

"Tell me about the loneliness of good,
He-Man. Is it equal to the loneliness of evil?"

Skeletor, *Masters of the Universe*, 1987

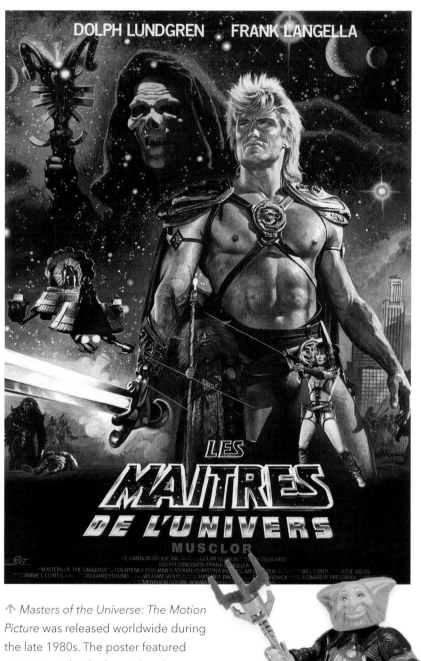

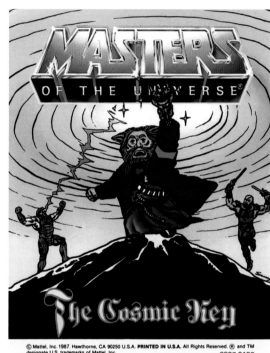

↑ *The Cosmic Key* minicomic came with movie-related toys Gwildor, Saurad, and "Evil Master of Swords," Blade. A malevolent force called the Evil Cloud creates Saurod and Blade and only Gwildor's Cosmic Key can defeat it.

↑ *Masters of the Universe: The Motion Picture* was released worldwide during the late 1980s. The poster featured stunning art by the legendary Drew Struzan, seen here in the French version.

→ Gwildor was created specially for the movie to provide comic relief as a substitute for Orko, whose floating design would have been too expensive to produce in live action.

Cosmic Key

Shoots sparks from mouth

Laser pistol

→ Saurod was a new character created for the film, a reptilian bounty hunter who worked for Skeletor. His toy, released in 1987, is shown here.

Creating Characters

At the start of the preproduction process for *Masters of the Universe*, director Gary Goddard brought in famed *Star Wars* concept artist Ralph McQuarrie. Having a prior commitment to work on another film, *Cocoon*, McQuarrie was only able to devote a matter of weeks to Goddard's movie. Together, they developed some initial ideas for Skeletor to wear a skull mask instead of actually being a talking skull being. Under the mask, his human face would be hideously scarred. In the end, they decided that Skeletor should remain an evil cackling skull monster, and the idea was dropped. As the main cast of characters began to be developed, likeness and costumes were initially based on the toys, but eventually gave way to new looks, most notably for Teela and Evil-Lyn. Budgetary limitations meant the director was not able to bring floating Orko or Battle Cat to the screen, so a new humanoid dwarflike character, Gwildor, was developed.

Simplified Snake Staff

Snake armor

MAN-AT-ARMS
Man-At-Arms, as visualized by Ralph McQuarrie, is recognizably inspired by the look of the classic toy, with tech-armor and green costume.

HE-MAN
Ralph McQuarrie visualized a naturalistic, relaxed He-Man in early development art. This artwork was created in 1984 as part of the initial pitch for the film.

TEELA
Teela's final costume in the movie would be completely reimagined from this concept art version by Ralph McQuarrie, which stayed faithful to the toy.

> ## "Ralph [McQuarrie] was in there at the very beginning."
>
> Gary Goddard, director, *Masters of the Universe*, 2012

SKELETOR

A full-length visualization of Skeletor by Italian artist
Claudio Mazzoli, who became the film's concept designer.

EVIL-LYN

McQuarrie's early artwork of Evil-Lyn closely
matches the design of the classic toy. Film
designer William Stout has said his final redesign
was inspired more by the Norma Desmond
character in Billy Wilder's *Sunset Boulevard*.

SKULL MASK

In this early study, Ralph
McQuarrie experiments with
making Skeletor a human
wearing a skull mask; the idea
was dropped for the final film.

↑ CASTLE GRAYSKULL
McQuarrie's visualization of Grayskull makes it much larger in proportion to the figures than it ever had been previously. In the final movie, the castle only featured in a single shot as a painting.

← GRAYSKULL SKETCH
A McQuarrie sketch reformats Castle Grayskull as a circular ruin, with the skull a smaller overall feature.

Visualizing the Setting

Masters of the Universe director Gary Goddard initially intended much of the film to be set on Eternia. He visualized the opening sequences as a montage of landscapes and aspects of the planet which would move inexorably toward Castle Grayskull. However, for budgetary reasons, these plans were scaled back and the decision was made to bring the Eternians to Earth—a more cost-effective approach, requiring fewer new sets to be built. The concept artwork, created by Ralph McQuarrie in just a few short weeks, gives a flavor of some of the early plans envisioned for Eternia. After McQuarrie moved onto *Cocoon*, William Stout came in, initially as key concept designer, then as production designer. Stout hired legendary French cartoonist Moebius (Jean Giraud) and Italian artist Claudio Mazzoli, who both contributed a great deal of new conceptual art for the movie.

↑ **PREWAR ETERNIA**
McQuarrie visualizes Eternia before the war, with moving sidewalks and waterways. Notes at the side call out the giant, domed trees.

← **DESOLATE ETERNIA**
Ralph McQuarrie visualized a plain of ashes on Eternia after the war, with rows of metal torches emitting blue flames lighting the way to the forbidding fortress of Castle Grayskull.

Unique Vehicles

Ralph McQuarrie produced some of the earliest sketches for vehicles for *Masters of the Universe: The Motion Picture*. Some of these, such as Skeletor's Air Centurions, were conceived in discussion with the director, Gary Goddard; they were not yet written into the script. "At this point I was still selling this idea to the producers and to the studio," said Goddard. "But Ralph got what I wanted right away." At first, ideas for vehicles were based on the existing Masters of the Universe toy line, but quickly the director and his concept artist began to explore new directions, wishing to give the film its own unique look. Goddard said, "We were in a world where sword and sorcery fantasy mixed freely with high-tech futuristic technology. We decided to take liberties, and yet find something new that would be based upon the world we were creating for the film and not on the preexisting toys. We came up with a mix of unique flying warships and air discs."

SMALL TANK
A design for a single-seater Attak Trak-like vehicle by Ralph McQuarrie.

AIR CENTURION
A McQuarrie study for Skeletor's Air Centurions. Director Gary Goddard said of McQuarrie's work, "There was a grace to the figures—he really had a great sense of staging and design."

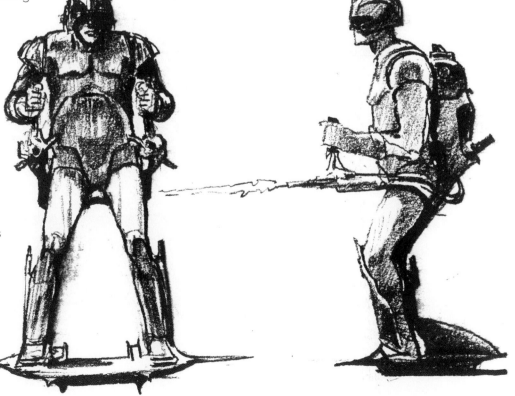

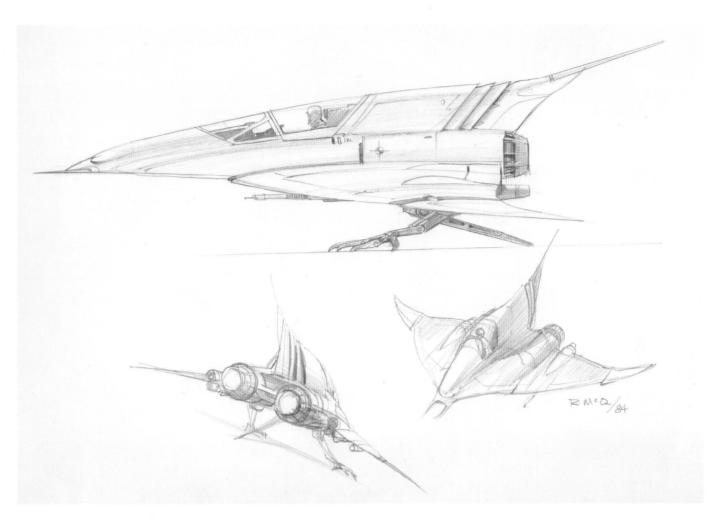

BEAKED FIGHTER
A McQuarrie early concept artwork for a vehicle inspired by the Talon Fighter, with a beak front and "claw" landing gear.

SCORPION WALKER
With this scorpion-inspired assault walker, McQuarrie begins to move away from designs based on existing toys and start creating vehicles from his own imagination.

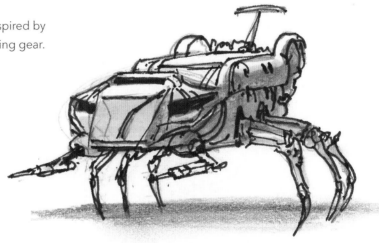

"[McQuarrie's] sketches, as simple as they were, helped me to sell the entire idea of the 'sky chase' between the Air Centurions and He-Man."

Gary Goddard, director, *Masters of the Universe*, 2012

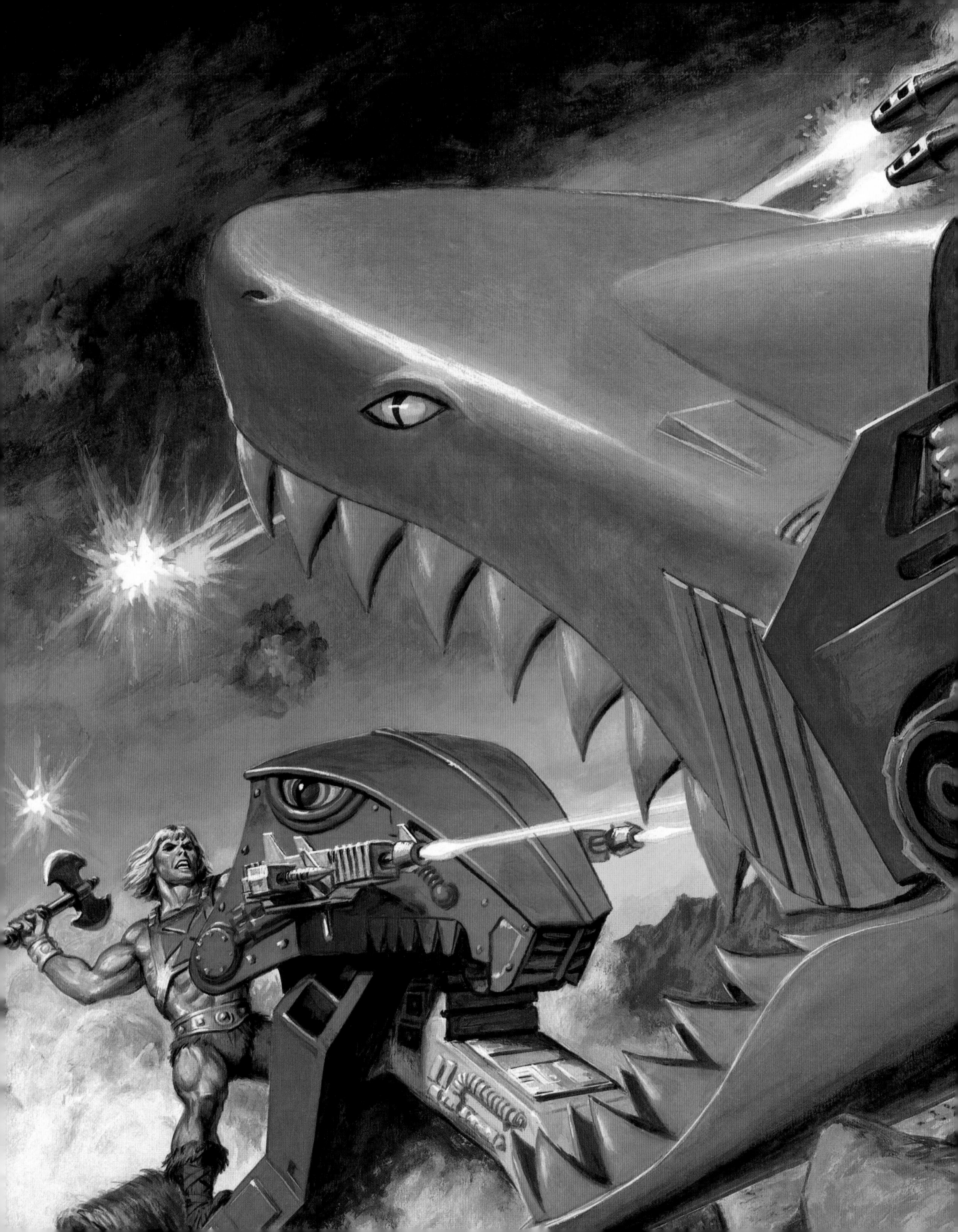

"High Adventure!
Exciting Action!
Spellbinding Magic!"

Tagline from Golden Storybooks (1983)

Magazine illustration by
Earl Norem *(left)* and
Golden Storybook cover
by Gino D'Achille *(below)*

THE POWER OF PRINT

DC Comics: 1980s

Mattel's partnership with DC Comics started back in the 1980s with minicomics and comic books.

From the start, He-Man and comic books were inextricably linked, with small-size comics being packaged with the action figures and vehicles. Mattel produced the first wave of four minicomics in 1982, but, for the second wave of toys which launched in 1983, Mattel worked with DC Comics. These seven comics were written by Gary Cohn and illustrated by Mark Texeira and Tod Smith, and featured characters such as Teela, Ram Man, Man-E-Faces, and Tri-Klops. Where the page layouts of the first wave of minicomics had been more picture book than comic strip, DC created dynamic comic-strip pages with panels and speech balloons. This run of comics significantly altered the course of Masters' history: Instead of the postapocalyptic Eternia of the first four comics, the planet is now a prosperous kingdom, with a King and Queen ruling from the palace. He-Man is no longer a wandering barbarian, but a member of the royal household, and Man-At-Arms becomes the adoptive father to Teela. He-Man and Skeletor each possess one half of the Power Sword, which must be placed together to allow ultimate power. In "The Menace of Trap Jaw," they even agree to join their swords in order to defeat a common enemy, Trap Jaw!

FULL-SIZE COMICS

In 1982, He-Man and Skeletor made the leap into two full-sized DC comic books, both one-shots, for adventures with Superman. The first, "From Eternia to Death," debuted in DC Comics Presents issue #47 in

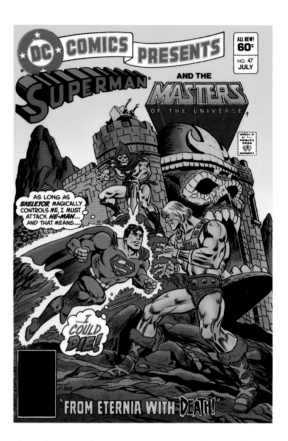

↑ In the one-shot crossover comic, from July 1982, Skeletor opens up a dimensional rift between Earth and Eternia and Superman is sucked through. Superman battles Skeletor and Beast Man—and even He-Man, after Skeletor uses magic to turn Superman against the Heroic Warriors. He-Man finally manages to return Superman to Earth.

July 1982, and was followed by "Fate is the Killer," inserted into a number of other DC Comics titles (a common promotional practice at the time). Next, a three-issue miniseries, written by Paul Kupperberg and pencilled by George Tuska, ran between December 1982 and February 1983. In these comics, we learn that Prince Adam is He-Man's alter ego. Instead of holding the Power Sword, however, he goes to the Cave of Power to transform. These comics began a partnership with DC Comics that would be revived in 2012.

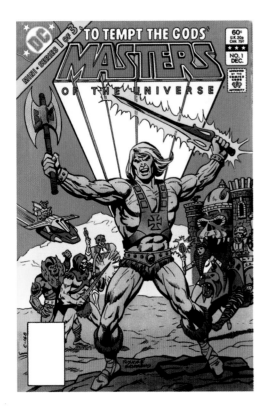

↑ The first of the three miniseries comics, "To Tempt the Gods," from December 1982, is a tale of demons unleashed by Skeletor and an ancient wizard named Tarrak, who lives in the Royal Palace—but will never be seen again.

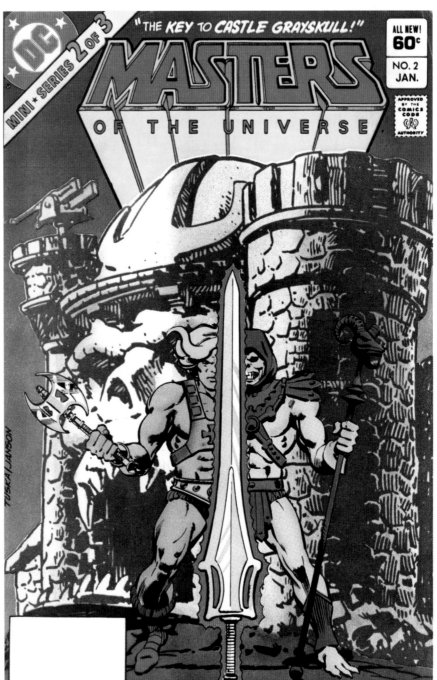

↑ Issue two of the three-part series, "The Key to Castle Grayskull," from January 1983, offers, among other events, a version of the first time Prince Adam becomes He-Man, aided by Zoar, in order to help a tribesman friend defend his village from a powerful sorcerer.

← In the third miniseries comic, from February 1983, Skeletor battles and defeats the powerful sorcerer Damon and manages to get inside Castle Grayskull. Within the walls of the castle, a climactic battle ensues against He-Man, Teela, and Battle Cat.

MASTERS OF THE UNIVERSE

CASTLE GRAYSKULL®
POINT DREAD™
ROAD RIPPER™
ZOAR®
FISTO™
TEELA®
WIND RAIDER®
STRIDOR™
ORKO™
MEKANECK™
BUZZ-OFF™
HE-MAN®
STRATOS®
DRAGON WALKER™
BATTLE ARMOR™ HE-MAN™
RAM-MAN®
SCREEECH™
PRINCE ADAM™
MAN-E-FACES®
MAN-AT-ARMS®
BATTLE CAT™

Artist William George created eye-catching box art paintings for many Masters of the Universe play sets and vehicles. Each year between 1984 and 1987, he also produced giveaway cross-sell posters, like this one from 1984, whose intricately constructed scenes display each year's range of toys, vehicles, and accessories.

Newspaper Strips

For four and a half years between 1986 and 1991, newspapers worldwide printed a syndicated He-Man comic strip. Initially written by Jim Shull and then by Chris Weber, the strip ran daily in black and white, drawn by Gerald Forton, and on Sundays in color, with color provided by Connie Schurr. The 15 storylines of the total run, each one unfolding over months, provide a continuation of the Filmation animated series and bridge the gap to *The New Adventures of He-Man* cartoon in 1990. In 2017, US publisher Dark Horse collected the entire run—except for a few "lost" strips—and published them in book form as *He-Man and the Masters of the Universe: The Newspaper Comic Strips*. Much of the art was recovered from microfilm, as the original art was missing and finding printed newspapers to scan was nearly impossible. For many fans, these strips were brand-new, as few saw the entire run at the time since many newspapers in the US had dropped the strip mid-run, though it continued to run in translation around the world.

↑ → A week's worth of strips from the 1987 storyline, "Vengeance Of The Viper King," shows He-Man vanquishing Hiss, the legendary leader of the Snake Men, then facing sneaky Skeletor—with plenty of quipping going on between the sword play!

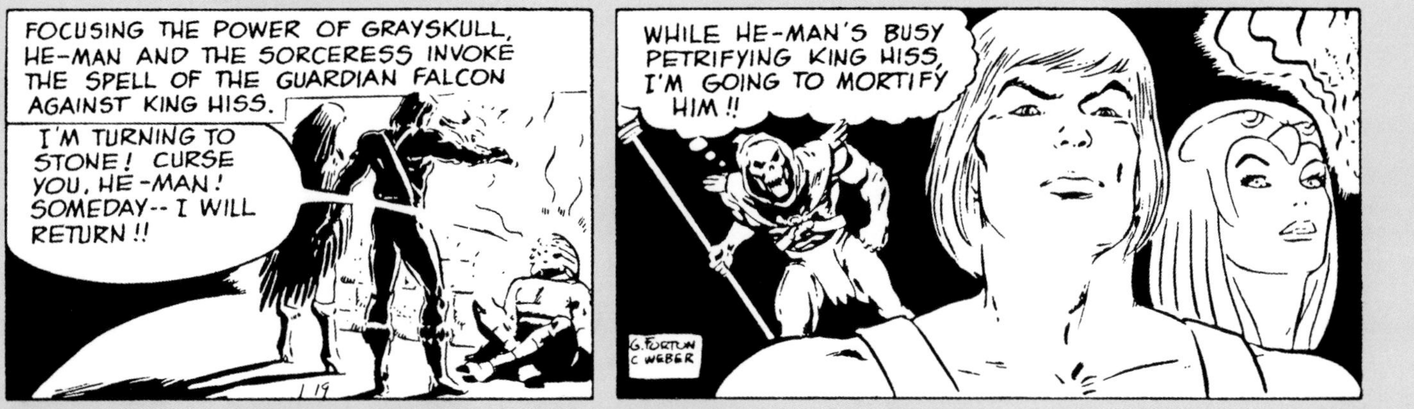
FOCUSING THE POWER OF GRAYSKULL, HE-MAN AND THE SORCERESS INVOKE THE SPELL OF THE GUARDIAN FALCON AGAINST KING HISS.
I'M TURNING TO STONE! CURSE YOU, HE-MAN! SOMEDAY-- I WILL RETURN!!
WHILE HE-MAN'S BUSY PETRIFYING KING HISS, I'M GOING TO MORTIFY HIM!!

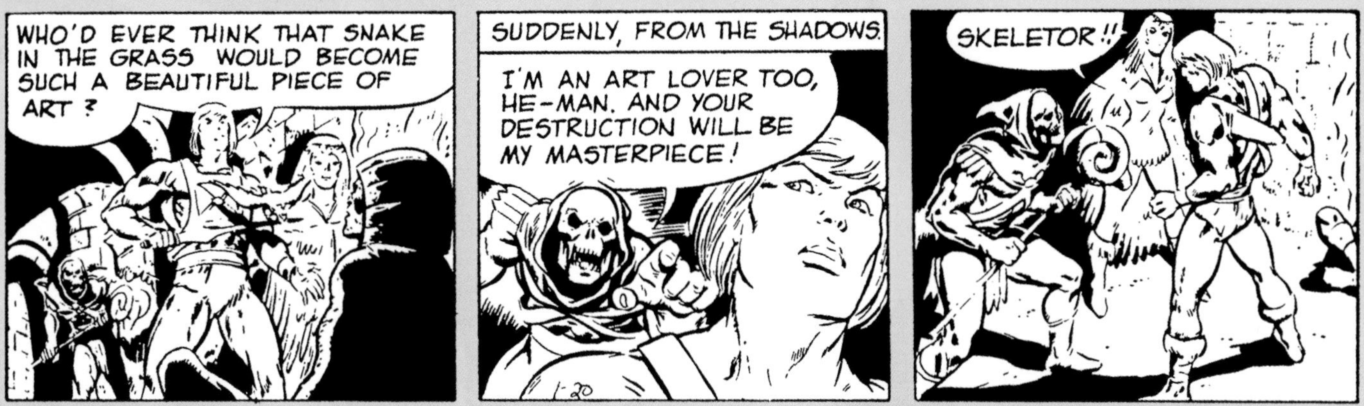
WHO'D EVER THINK THAT SNAKE IN THE GRASS WOULD BECOME SUCH A BEAUTIFUL PIECE OF ART ?
SUDDENLY, FROM THE SHADOWS.
I'M AN ART LOVER TOO, HE-MAN. AND YOUR DESTRUCTION WILL BE MY MASTERPIECE!
SKELETOR!!

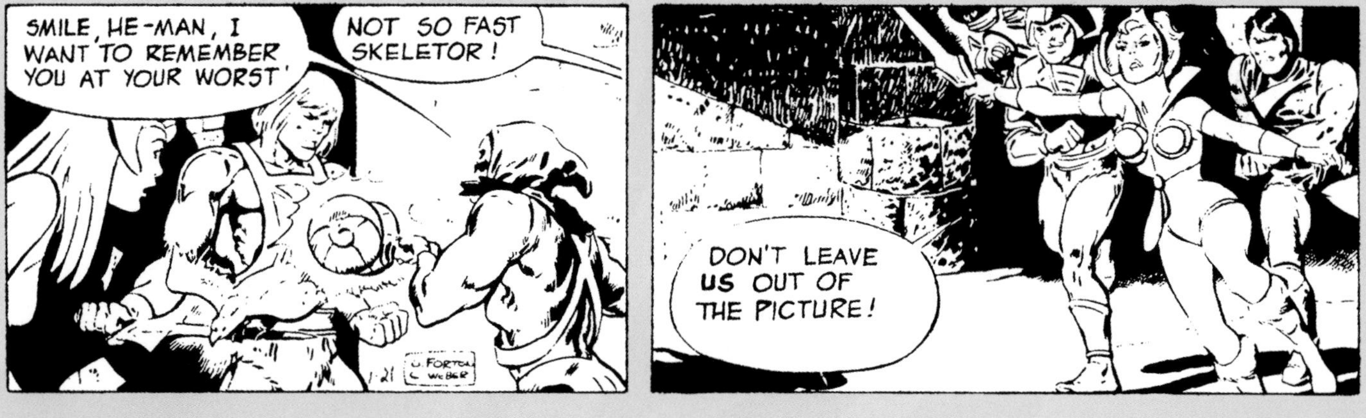
SMILE, HE-MAN, I WANT TO REMEMBER YOU AT YOUR WORST'
NOT SO FAST SKELETOR!
DON'T LEAVE **US** OUT OF THE PICTURE!

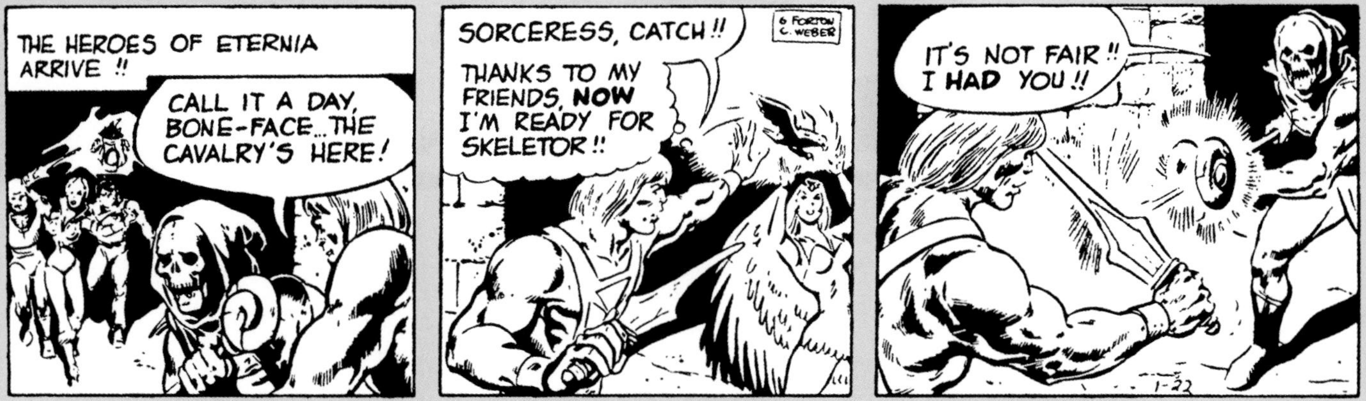
THE HEROES OF ETERNIA ARRIVE!!
CALL IT A DAY, BONE-FACE...THE CAVALRY'S HERE!
SORCERESS, CATCH!!
THANKS TO MY FRIENDS, **NOW** I'M READY FOR SKELETOR!!
IT'S NOT FAIR!! I **HAD** YOU!!

Masters of the Universe Publishing

In the 1980s, Golden Books in the US led the way in print publishing for He-Man and the Masters of the Universe, producing a wide range of illustrated picture books, activity books, and more. In the UK, Ladybird issued fiction and novelty formats—including an "Action Frieze" which told the He-Man story in pictures, ready for hanging on a bedroom wall. Ladybird also worked with Pickwick Records to produce read-along book-and-cassette sets; Kid Stuff Records made similar products in the US. World International (part of the publisher Egmont) distributed yearly MOTU Annuals between 1984 and 1990, which featured a variety of comic strips, photographic content, puzzles, and more. Internationally, Masters of the Universe books were published in Germany, Italy, France, and elsewhere.

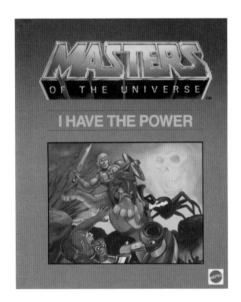

ORIGIN STORY
I Have the Power tells He-Man's origin story and features a rare appearance from the Council of Elders, who imbued Castle Grayskull with all their powers.

STOP THE CLOCK
Time Trouble, published by Golden Storybooks in 1984, features dynamic cover art by Earl Norem, showing He-Man trying to stop the Cosmic Clock.

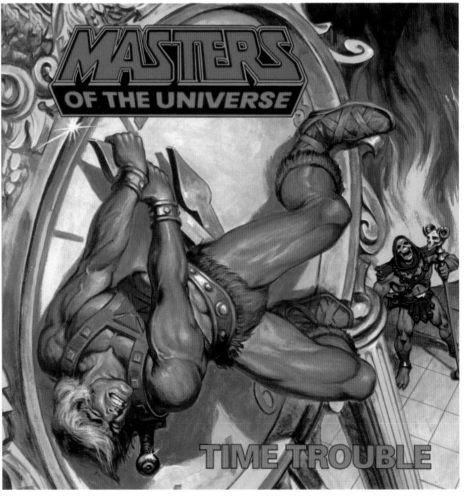

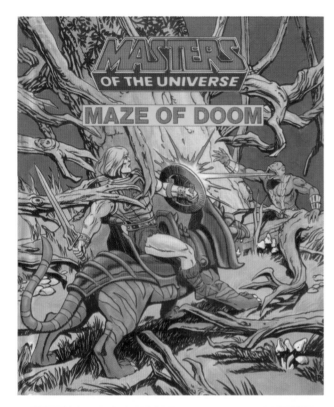

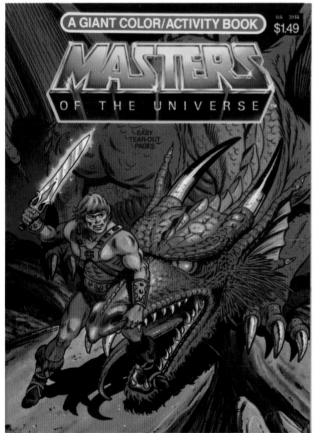

SKELETOR'S MAZE

Released in 1985 in the Golden Heroic Champions series, *Maze of Doom* sees He-Man and the Heroic Warriors trying to free themselves from Skeletor's magical maze, which he has caused to grow up around the Royal Palace.

EVIL WARRIORS

This 24-page large-format book from Golden includes 12 full-color illustrations by Filipino comics artist Fred Carillo (who also worked on titles for Marvel and DC Comics) and pages of facts about Skeletor, Beast Man, Evil-Lyn, and others.

DRAGON QUEST

The striking cover art for this Golden Books title is by American fantasy artist Larry Elmore, whose work includes illustrations for *Dungeons & Dragons*.

THE LAKE OF MYSTERY

There is a strange lake on Eternia called the Lake of Mystery. Things look different when they're reflected in *this* lake! Circle the 17 things that are wrong in the reflection.

Illustration by Earl Norem.

In the 1980s, artist Earl Norem created many large illustrations, often designed as foldout posters, for magazines. This particular piece, The Lake of Mystery, appeared in issue six of *He-Man and the Masters of the Universe Magazine*, dated Spring 1986. It highlights the range of toys available at the time and includes a puzzle element: spot the things that look wrong in the reflection.

Princess of Power Publishing

She-Ra leaped into book aisles in the 1980s with a wide range of titles from publishers such as Golden Books and Ladybird, including fiction, activity, coloring, and sticker albums. Novelty formats included paper-doll books, paint-with-water books, and read-along book-and-cassette sets. *She-Ra: Princess of Power Magazine* ran for six issues between 1986 and 1987, featuring a range of original stories and pull-out posters.

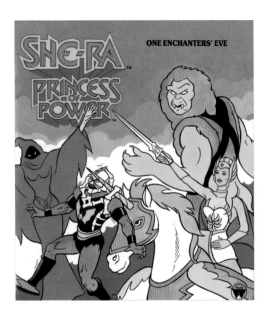

STORY BOOK
This story book, published in 1986 by World in the UK, includes two stories: "One Enchanter's Eve," about Shadow Weaver's growth potion, and "Battle for Bright Moon."

POWER POSTER
One of two posters that came with *She-Ra: Princess of Power Magazine* issue #1 in 1986, this colorful grouping shows the full range of characters from the first year, with Crystal Castle in the background, featuring the toy set with the golden tower from the animated series on top of it.

"The Princess of Power gathers her glamorous friends at Crystal Castle."

She-Ra: Princess of Power Magazine, issue 1, 1986

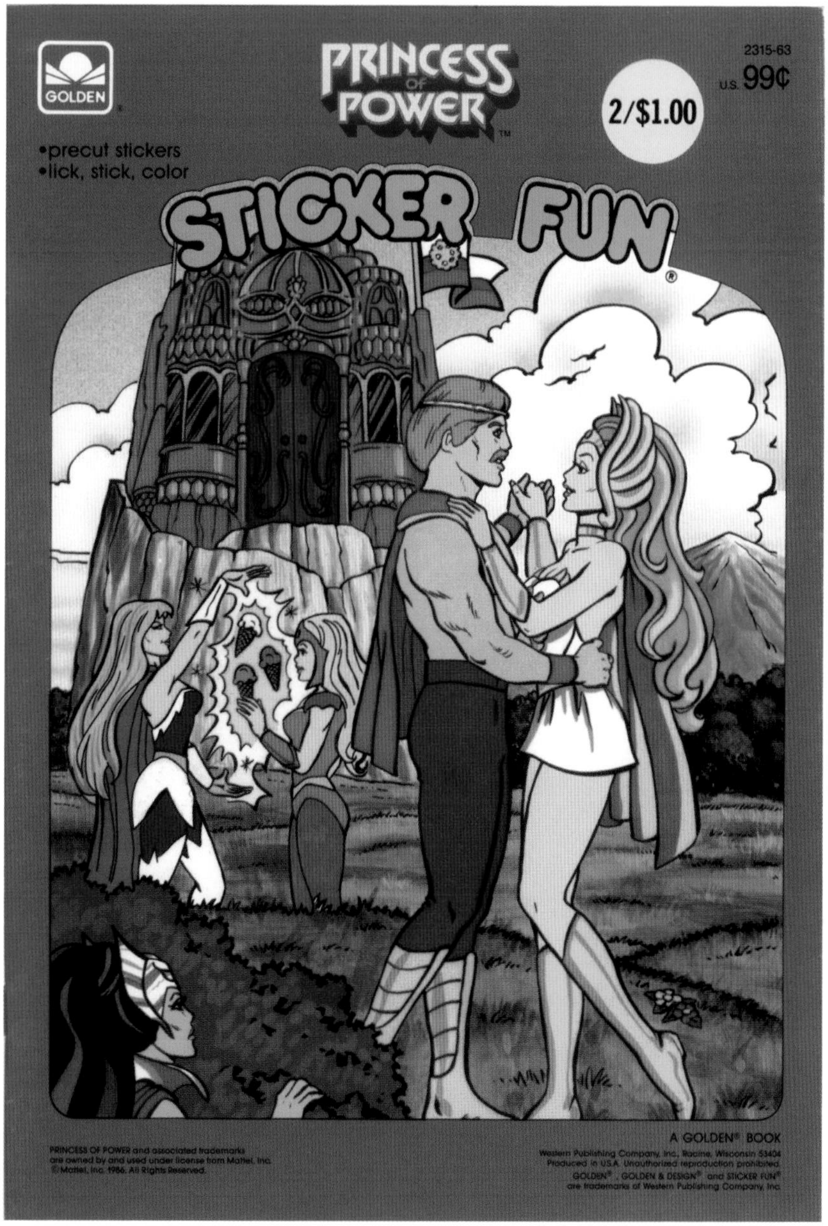
GOLDEN
PRINCESS OF POWER
2315-63
U.S. 99¢
2/$1.00
•precut stickers
•lick, stick, color
STICKER FUN
A GOLDEN® BOOK

STICKER FUN

This 16-page sticker book from 1986 features a mix of press-out Princess of Power character stickers and coloring pages, with a door sign featuring a grouping of She-Ra and friends, whch can be cut out from the back cover and tied to a bedroom doorknob.

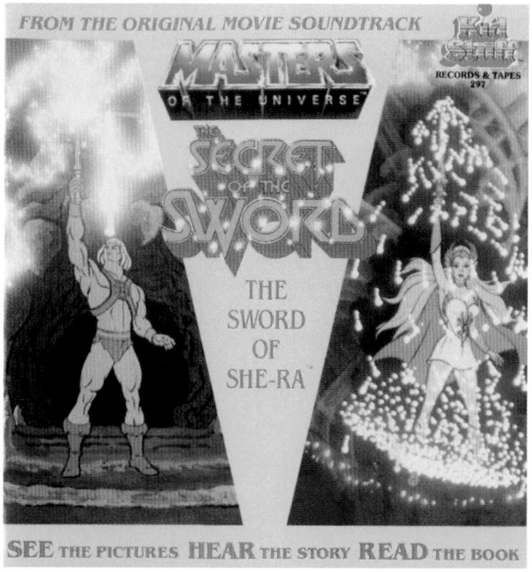
FROM THE ORIGINAL MOVIE SOUNDTRACK
MASTERS OF THE UNIVERSE
THE SECRET OF THE SWORD
RECORDS & TAPES
297
THE SWORD OF SHE-RA
SEE THE PICTURES HEAR THE STORY READ THE BOOK

MOVIE RETELLING

In 1985, Kid Stuff issued two books that retold *The Secret of the Sword* using stills from the movie. The read-along versions came with either a vinyl record or a cassette tape.

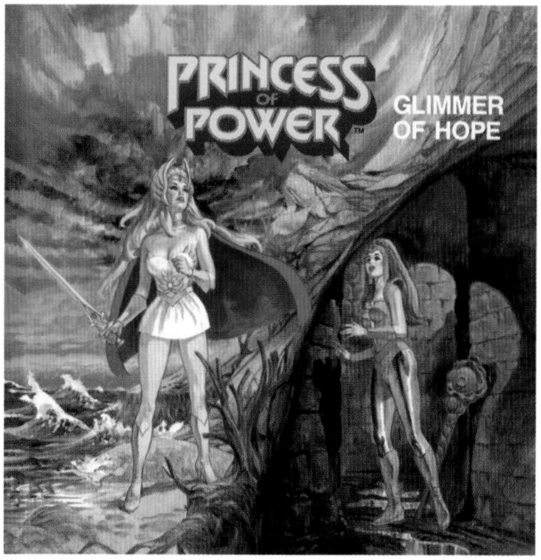
PRINCESS OF POWER
GLIMMER OF HOPE

ADVENTURE BOOK

Glimmer of Hope is a Golden Super Adventure title published in 1985, with a cover by Spanish comic book artist Fernando Fernández.

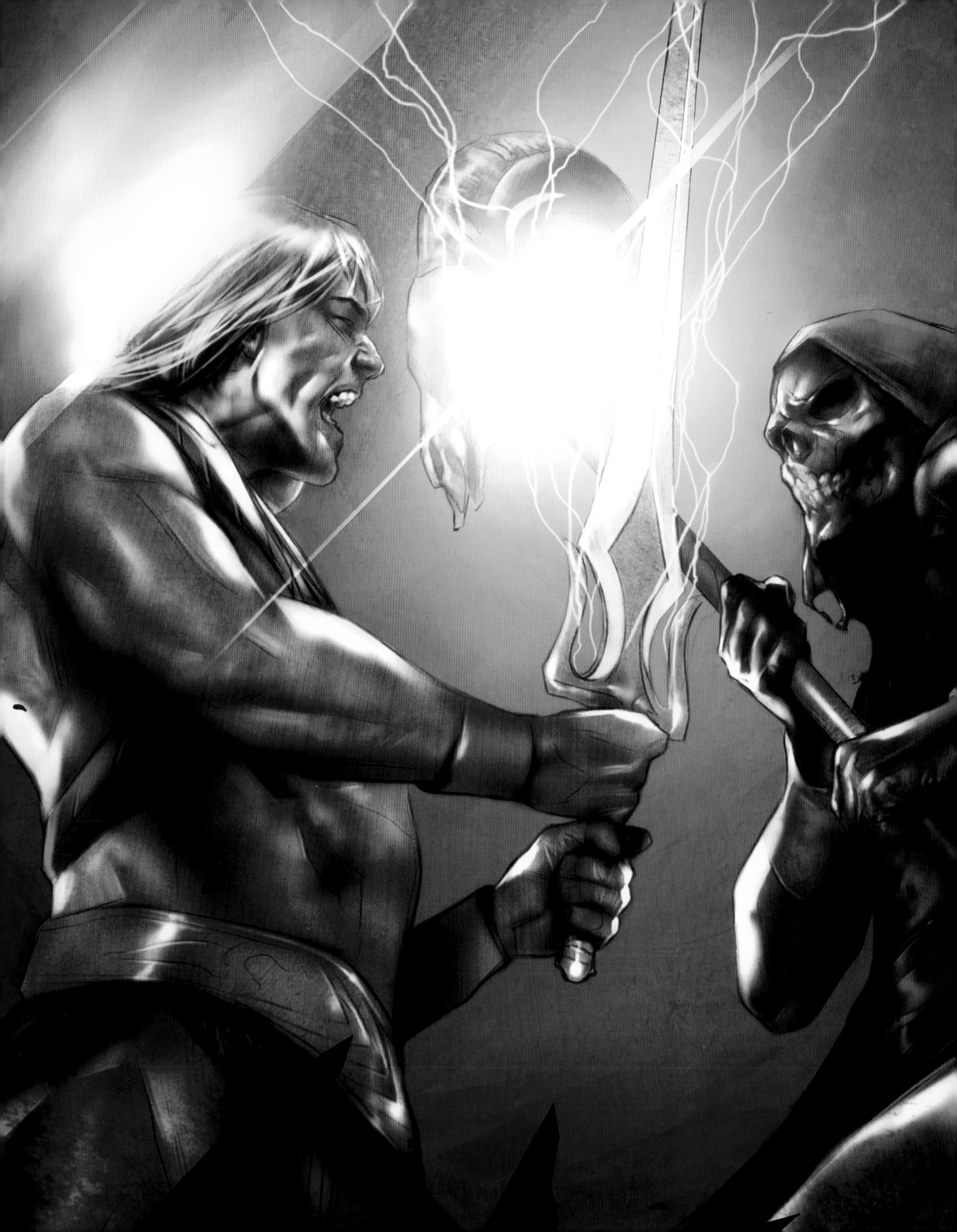

HE-MAN RETURNS

"We just kind of came along at the exact right time."

H. Eric "Cornboy" Mayse, co-founder, Four Horsemen Studios, 2021

Interior art from DC Comics' *The Origin of He-Man (left)* and Stratos action figure from Four Horsemen *(below)*

The New Adventures of He-Man

He-Man is back! This time, he's the futuristic defender of the planet Primus.

In the animated TV series, *The New Adventures of He-Man*, which debuted in 1990, He-Man is summoned to the futuristic planet of Primus to defend it from the evil Mutants of the neighboring planet of Denebria. However, his old adversary Skeletor has followed him and allied himself with the leader of the Mutants, Commander Flogg. Together with a team of Galactic Guardians, He-Man fights to defend Primus and all its power resources from attacks by Skeletor and the Mutants. The new show introduces new warriors from Primus, including Hydron, Flipshot, and Kayo. Among the few new female characters is a trainee sorceress named Mara. The Mutants, led by Flogg, include amphibious Slush Head, eyeball-headed Optikk, and a variant on Ram Man crossed with Mekaneck named Butthead!

DEVELOPMENT

The relaunch had been in development since 1986, with the creators of the original series, Filmation, pitching at least two concepts for a new show: *Son of He-Man* and *He-Man and the Masters of Space*. However, when Filmation was sold and then closed in 1989, Mattel partnered with a new animation company, Jetlag Productions, which produced 65 episodes of the new show.

H.E/M.A.N.

HIGH ENERGY MILITARY ATTACK NUCLEUS

← One of the early concepts for the new show was a futuristic military theme called H.E.M.A.N., as seen in this concept art created by Mattel designer Dave McElroy.

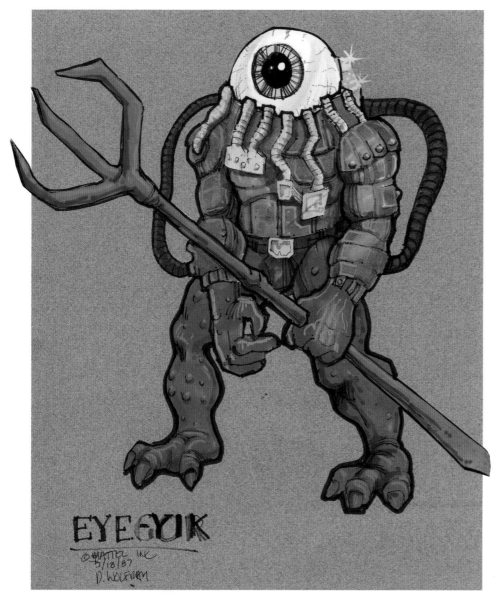

EYE-YIK

↑ He-Man wields a lightsaber-style Power Sword and high-tech shield, in concept art by designer Martin Arriola, who worked on the original toy line.

↑ Mattel designer David Wolfram's early design for Optikk, named "Eye-Yik," has a trident and a ring of power feeds connecting his eyeball head to his cyborg suit.

← The initial releases in the new toy line matched the original toy line with a range of minicomics.

BIO-MECHAZOID SKELETOR

↑ The animators on the TV show used concept art for the toys as inspiration, such as this art of Laser-Light Skeletor.

He-Man Action Figures

Mattel's new toy line, called simply He-Man, debuted in 1989 and featured characters from *The New Adventures of He-Man* animated series. The toys were less muscle-heavy than the classic line, allowing them to more easily sit in vehicles, though some of the later variants were more beefed up. The heroic Galactic Guardians, such as Flipshot, Kayo, and Hydron, are humanoid and less weird-looking than most of the original Heroic Warriors (with the exception of Tuskador!). But the Mutants more than make up for this in strangeness: green-faced Hoove with his high-kicking action; brutal-looking Karatti; and, best of all, Optikk, with a giant eyeball for a head! Many had action features: Artilla's face springs forward for a "head butt" and Butthead's head shoots upward—this toy's initial design was by Mark Taylor, one of the original creators of the classic toy line. Key characters were issued in fun variations, such as Disks of Doom Skeletor with his throwing disk action and real glowing red eyes.

Psychotronic disk launcher

DISKS OF DOOM SKELETOR

Skull Staff

Translucent Sword of Power

Beefed-up muscles

SKELETOR　　　BATTLE BLADE SKELETOR　　　HE-MAN　　　ROCKET DISK

BUTTHEAD　　　TUSKADOR　　　VIZAR　　　THUNDER PUNCH HE-MAN

SPINWIT

OPTIKK

SAGITAR

Running knuckles

HYDRON

Removable scuba dome

NOCTURNA

STAGHORN

Mechanical antlers

TOO-TALL HOOVE

SLUSH HEAD

KARATTI

FLIPSHOT

KAYO

Energy whip

FLOGG

HOOVE

Grabatron Meteormace

QUAKKE

ARTILLA

LIZORR

He-Man Vehicles and Play Sets

The first year of He-Man toys in 1989 includes several small vehicles, including the Terrorclaw, Bolajet, and Astrosub, but the stand-out set is Starship Eternia. It is a large spaceship, with opening cockpit, rotating blasters, and lights and sounds. The back of the box shows the 12 different modes of transformation, including Command Center, Space Station, Deep Space Probe, Science Lab, and Communications Satellite. In 1990, the highlight from the second wave of toys is Nordor, the Evil Mutants' lair, which stands comparison to the classic Castle Grayskull set in the original MOTU toy line. It features a throne for Skeletor—the first ever in a toy set—and a working projector with film strips for projecting images of He-Man and his allies onto the large, white screen in the middle of the play set or onto a bedroom wall.

← Nordor is the skull-shaped moon of the planet Denebria that forms the main headquarters of Flogg and his Mutants. The toy set folds closed to resemble a purple asteroid with a skull face.

Space weapon

Projector screen

Asteroid mode

Seat for action figure

← Terrortread, from 1991, is Skeletor's bird-faced all-terrain assault vehicle, which can transform into different stalking modes for ultimate menace: watch out Galactic Guardians!

Magna-blaster

Tank treads

Opening cockpit

← In the animated series, Flipshot and Hydron use Starship Eternia to travel back in time in their search for He-Man. The set can be reconfigured in 12 different ways, including opening up to form Ground Base Command.

Elevator shaft

Rip-rotor projectile

← Skeletor's Doomcopter toy, released in 1991, features a handle on the back that can be held to swoosh the vehicle into the air; triggers on the handle make the jaws chomp up and down and can launch the bladed propeller from the top.

Trapdoor hidden on underside of cockpit

Grabber claw

Wheel treads

↑ The Terrorclaw, from 1989, has three modes: body horizontal (with a cockpit for Skeletor), body upright, and kneeling down as a tank.

ORKO

WAR WHALE

Battle ax

New "techno-style"
Power Sword

2002 Relaunch

After a decade of hibernation, He-Man was ready for a rebirth. It began in 2000 with the Commemorative Series: reissues of the classic toys with larger box windows and reprints of the minicomics. Then, at San Diego Comic-Con in 2001, Mattel announced their collaboration with toy designers Four Horsemen Studios. Toy production technology had advanced massively in the decade since the 1989-1992 He-Man line, and Four Horsemen Studios is famed for its innovative, highly intricate designs and sculpts. The team are also long-time MOTU admirers, adding fan-level details inspired by their deep love of the original toys, such as Hordak-inspired bat symbols on the back of Skeletor's legs to hint at his backstory as Hordak's apprentice. While Four Horsemen Studios focused on the characters, Mattel produced a range of new vehicles with a similar aesthetic, including a new version of the classic Battle Bones and an updated Castle Grayskull. With seven waves of toys released between 2002 and 2004, the new designs changed the look of the toys and influenced the animated TV series that debuted alongside them. As Eric Treadaway, one of the four founders of the studio, said in 2015, "To this day we are still floored that we were given so much artistic freedom on the line."

HE-MAN

NEW CASTS
The toys in the Commemorative Series were made from casts of the actual vintage action figures since the original molds were no longer usable.

Magic staff

Loose hair
replaces
classic bun

TEELA

EVIL-LYN

Bright gold
styling on
battle outfit

Silver ram's
head on
Havoc Staff

New purple
styling

Enlarged right
boot allows for
Action Chip
feature

Head can be swapped
for Skeletor's head

Vial of
green acid

Dual-bladed
sword

SKELETOR

KELDOR

Relaunched Animation and Comic Books

The relaunched toy line from Four Horsemen Studios in 2002 brought with it a new animated series and comic-book series. The last time He-Man was seen on TV screens, in *The New Adventures of He-Man* a decade earlier, he was on the futuristic planet Primus with his team of Galactic Guardians. Now he returns to Eternia and the core characters from the original series are reintroduced, including King Randor, the Sorceress, Man-At-Arms, Teela, Orko, and Prince Adam—still seemingly spoiled and carefree, discovering all over again that he has the power. In season one, Skeletor convenes a grand council of evil warriors and Evil-Lyn is her usual deceitful self. Season two sees King Hiss and the Snake Men rising to prominence. The accompanying comic-book series, created by MVCreations and published by Image Comics, targeted slightly older fans than the show and featured a wide range of characters and art styles. "Masters itself is a cornucopia of different characters and story concepts," said series producer Val Staples. "I felt the comic should represent that."

ANIMATED ADVENTURES
First aired on Cartoon Network in 2002 and running until 2004, the new animated series reunites the original Heroic Warriors, including favorites Stratos and Ram Man. Fisto also appears in the show as Man-At-Arms' long-lost brother.

INTO BATTLE
He-Man grasps the updated Sword of Power in cover artwork by Keron Grant, Pierre-André Déry, and Val Staples, from issue four of the comic-book series, *Masters of the Universe* Vol. 1 ("The Shards of Darkness") released in 2003.

UPDATED MENACE
Four Horsemen Studios created new concept artwork for Mantenna.

ORIGIN STORY
The jaw-smashing punch that turns a renegade criminal into Trap Jaw: a panel from the *Icons of Evil: Trap Jaw* comic that was published in 2003 and written by Robert Kirkman, creator of *The Walking Dead*.

SKELETOR
Skeletor holds He-Man's captured Power Sword, in artwork by Four Horsemen Studios. In the final story, He-Man carries a new, redesigned sword.

Classics Toy Line

Four Horsemen Studios create the largest-ever range of Masters action figures with Classics.

As the 2002 action-figure line was coming to an end, Four Horsemen Studio's next move was to partner with collectibles manufacturer NECA to release larger statues and busts, as well as a series of smaller mini-statues. Created in the same scale as the action figures but without articulation, the mini-statues became known as "stactions" (static action figures).

MOTU CLASSICS

At San Diego Comic-Con in 2007, Four Horsemen Studios showed Mattel a prototype design they had made for He-Man. Right away, Mattel put it on display at the show, generating huge interest from fans. A year later, the first Masters of the Universe Classics action figure, King Grayskull, was released at the 2008 San Diego Comic-Con. The new line went back to the original 1980s toys for its look and feel, now with greater detail and points of articulation. The Four Horsemen designers and sculptors updated many action figures from the original line and made figures for characters that had never appeared before, including Queen Marlena and Lizard-Man. They also released characters from the original minicomics, *She-Ra: Princess of Power*, *The New Adventures of He-Man*, and the 2002 *He-Man and the Masters of the Universe* animated series, as well as some newly invented characters.

→ The mini-statue of the Sorceress was released in 2006 as an exclusive from online retailer AFX.

Gold armor

Wizard staff

↑ He-Ro is modeled on a prototype figure made for a canceled toy line intended to follow the original MOTU toys in the 1980s.

Sword of Power (in two halves, with Skeletor)

→ He-Man kicked off the line in 2008. Like most of the Classics figures, action features have given way to detailed sculpts and better articulation.

MINING THE LORE

Fan-favorite prototypes and concept art were also turned into figures, starting with the 2009 San Diego Comic-Con exclusive He-Ro (the proposed hero of a canceled spin-off line, "The Powers of Grayskull," from 1987) and including Demo-Man and Vykor (both from early Mark Taylor concept art). Intended initially as a short-term line, MOTU Classics ultimately ran for longer than the original line: since 2008, more than 250 action figures have been released—and that's not including all the beasts, giants, vehicles, and play sets!

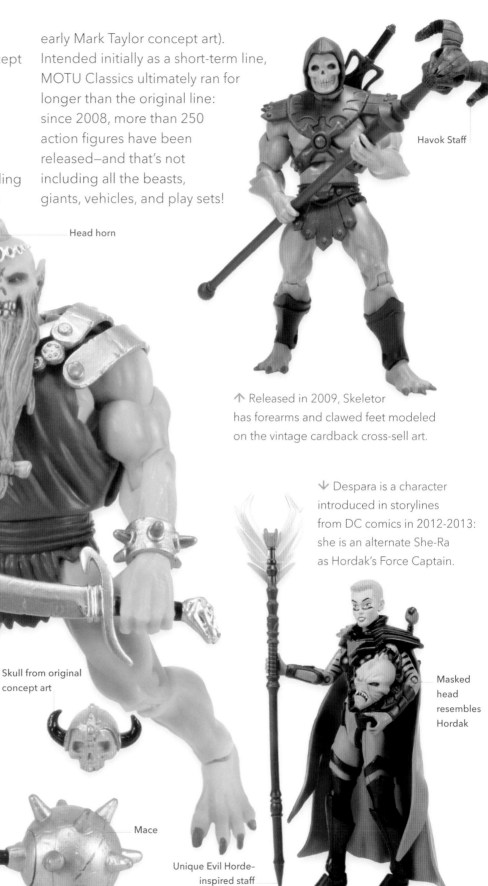

Havok Staff

→ Demo-Man is modeled on a concept originally thought to be for Skeletor, created by Mattel designer Mark Taylor in the early 1980s.

Head horn

Cutlass

Skull from original concept art

Mace

↑ Released in 2009, Skeletor has forearms and clawed feet modeled on the vintage cardback cross-sell art.

↓ Despara is a character introduced in storylines from DC comics in 2012-2013: she is an alternate She-Ra as Hordak's Force Captain.

Masked head resembles Hordak

Unique Evil Horde–inspired staff

New mold for flag

Minaret from Mark
Taylor prototype model

Laser turret

Skull sculpt
more closely
matches Mark
Taylor's original

Lockable
jawbridge is
8 inches (20 cm)
in height

New sculpt for training device

ULTIMATE FORTRESS
This play set stands nearly 2 feet (61 cm) tall and
includes details from the original Grayskull prototype
model made by designer Mark Taylor in the 1980s.

Castle Grayskull 2013

I n 2013, Castle Grayskull was updated for the
MOTU Classics line, funded partially by fans
through a presale campaign. Four Horsemen
Studios created concept art to show a range of
possible ideas, including a transparent "Spirit of
Grayskull" piece to clip onto the top, inspired by
one of the illustrations in the first wave of
minicomics in the 1980s. The model was then
rendered in resin with four detailed walls and a
fully realized roof. The designers used Mattel's
original Grayskull play set from 1982 as
inspiration but brought in a new level of detail.

EARLY CONCEPT

A design for the exterior, showing the ghostly Spirit of Grayskull piece that was considered.

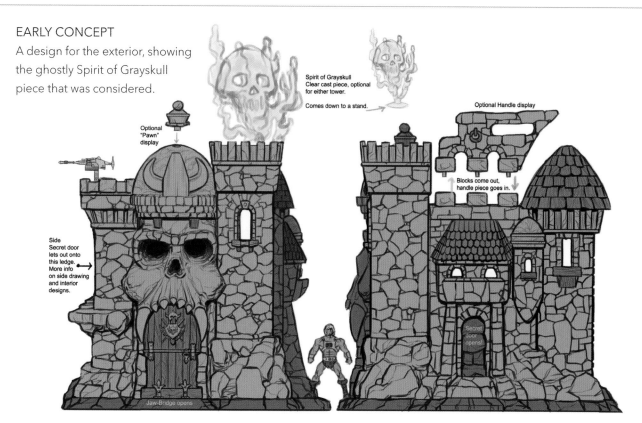

Spirit of Grayskull
Clear cast piece, optional for either tower.

Comes down to a stand.

Optional "Pawn" display

Optional Handle display

Blocks come out, handle piece goes in.

Side Secret door lets out onto this ledge. More info on side drawing and interior designs.

Secret door opens!

Jaw-Bridge opens

INTERIOR DESIGNS

Some concept art produced by Four Horsemen Studios was used in modified form to promote the presale campaign.

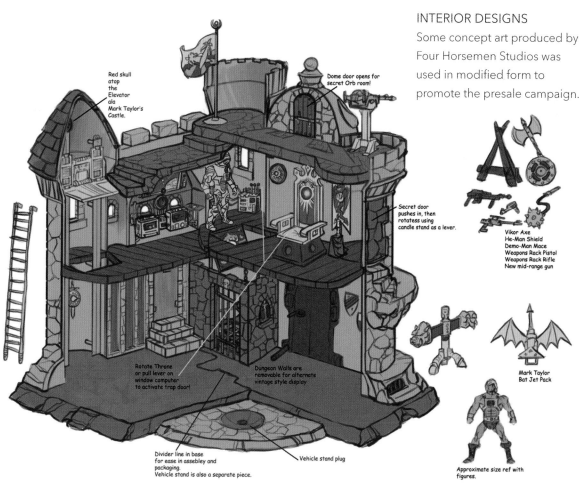

Red skull atop the Elevator ala Mark Taylor's Castle.

Dome door opens for secret Orb room!

Secret door pushes in, then rotatess using candle stand as a lever.

Rotate Throne or pull lever on window computer to activate trap door!

Dungeon Walls are removable for alternate vintage style display.

Divider line in base for ease in assebley and packaging. Vehicle stand is also a separate piece.

Vehicle stand plug

Vikor Axe
He-Man Shield
Demo-Man Mace
Weapons Rack Pistol
Weapons Rack Rifle
New mid-range gun

Mark Taylor Bat Jet Pack

Approximate size ref with figures.

Collectible He-Man

The He-Man toy line that tied into *The New Adventures of He-Man* in 1989-1992 featured the first Mattel-released role-play toys, including the Power Sword and Skeletor's Skull Staff. Previously, these toys had been made by other companies—these were the first official ones as part of the Mattel toy line. The Power Sword is powered by Grayskull … well, really by batteries, creating laser and thunder sound effects, and a light-up blade. Skeletor's Skull Staff features various sound and light effects, including Skeletor's evil laugh and eyes that glow red. In 2002, the relaunched Masters of the Universe animation and toy line saw a wide array of merchandise, including watches, sunglasses, key chains, and … toothbrushes of power! More recent Masters merchandise will become the sought-after collectibles of tomorrow, such as Baby Skeletor, a 12-inch (30-cm) figure that comes with a Havoc Staff rattle, a "Born to Rule" baby t-shirt, and a throne (in the form of an "evil royal potty")!

1

2

3

4

5

6

7

9

8

10

11

12   13

14

1 **He-Man Powersword,** Mattel (1989)
2 **Baby Skeletor,** Mattel (2014)
3 **He-Man toy and cassette gift pack,** Mattel (1989)
4 **He-Man and the Masters of the Universe celebration banner,** Hallmark (2000s)
5 **He-Man and the Masters of the Universe keychain,** Basic Fun (2002)
6 **He-Man and the Masters of the Universe sunglasses** (2003)
7 **He-Man and the Masters of the Universe AirHeads Xtremes candy,** Perfetti Van Melle (2000s)
8 **Skeletor Skull Staff,** Mattel (1991)
9 **He-Man Electronic Thunder Punch,** Mattel (1992)
10 *I Am He-Man!* Little Golden Books (2020)
11 **He-Man watch** (2000s)
12 **Masters of the Universe toothbrush,** Colgate (2000s)
13 **Skeletor toothpaste,** Colgate (2000s)
14 **Masters of the Universe: The Snake Men sssnake disk shooter,** Premium World (2004)

DC Comics: New Stories

In 2012, DC Comics and Mattel are reunited with the launch of new comic books.

Creative directed by Rob David, Executive Producer, Mattel Television, the collaboration kicks off in June 2012 with digital comics featuring standalone stories about characters such as Battle Cat; Man-At-Arms; and a brand-new knight from Eternia's prehistory, Sir Laser-Lot. The comics tie into a six-issue miniseries, *He-Man and the Masters of the Universe* in which Skeletor takes control of Castle Grayskull and murders the Sorceress.

INTO THE ETERNITY WAR

In 2013, a second, ongoing series debuts with an invasion of the Horde led by Despara, who is Teela's childhood friend Adora, destined to become She-Ra. In the second story arc, King Randor leads He-Man and his allies into Subternia in an attempt to bring the Sorceress back to life—where they face the reborn Snake Men. The third arc explores the origin of She-Ra and leads into *He-Man: The Eternity War*, which runs for 15 issues between 2015 and 2016. Written and developed by Rob David, adapted into comic book-script format by Dan Abnett, with art by Pop Mhan, this epic series presents new origin stories and shows both Teela fulfilling her destiny as the new Sorceress and He-Man ascending to the Eternian throne. Many story elements and designs from *He-Man: The Eternity War* provided inspiration for *Masters of the Universe: Revelation*, the 2021 Netflix animated series.

CROSSOVERS AND MORE

In 2013, He-Man appears in a six-issue crossover series with DC Comics' the Justice League and, in

↑ DC Comics CCO Geoff Johns created Sir Laser-Lot when he was 8 years old. In 2012, Laser-Lot debuted in the *Masters of the Universe* issue #1, and later became an action figure.

2016, a miniseries with fellow 1980s action heroes ThunderCats. In a further crossover series, He-Man is called on to help defeat a villainous Superman in DC Comics' alternative-reality Injustice storyline. In 2019, He-Man enters the multiverse in *He-Man and the Masters of the Multiverse*, recruiting Prince Keldor—the future Skeletor—in a final desperate battle.

↑ Front cover art from *He-Man and the Masters of the Multiverse* issue #4, in which He-Man and Keldor travel back to the Eternia of the Filmation TV series.

↑ An epic clash on the front cover of *He-Man: The Eternity War* vol. #1 from 2015, with art by Stjepan Sejic.

→ As seen on the cover of *He-Man and the Masters of the Universe* issue #2 from 2013, Despara is Adora's evil alter ego and the Force Captain of the Evil Horde.

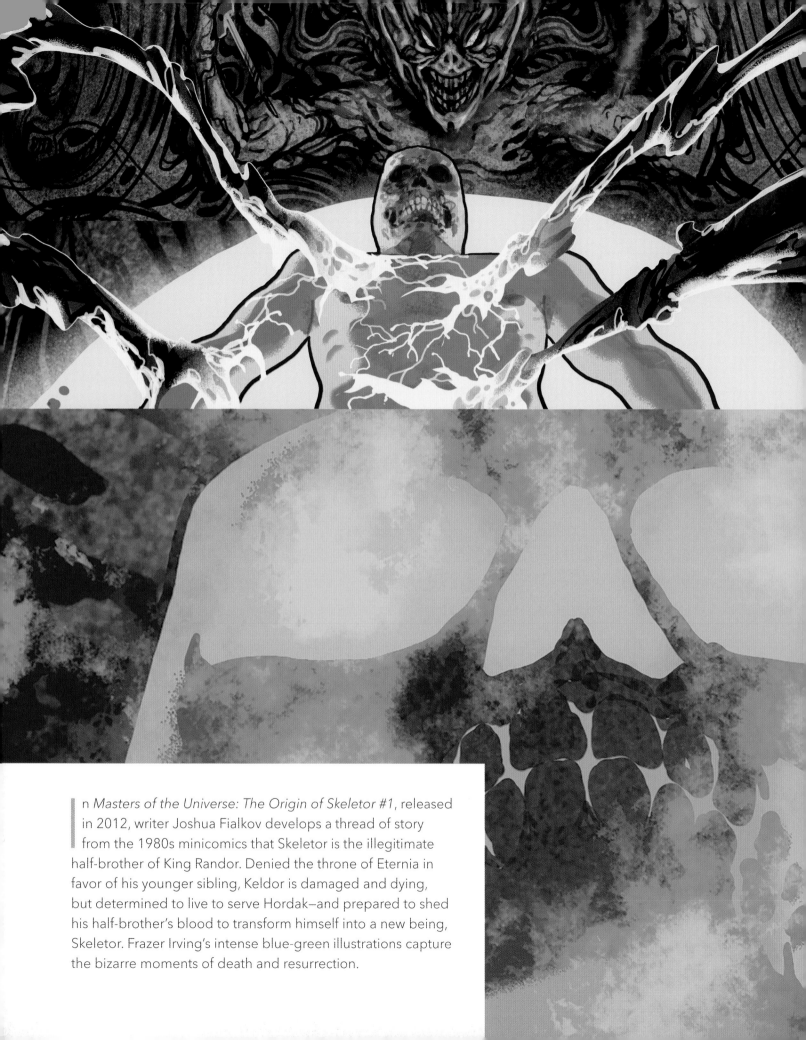

n *Masters of the Universe: The Origin of Skeletor #1*, released in 2012, writer Joshua Fialkov develops a thread of story from the 1980s minicomics that Skeletor is the illegitimate half-brother of King Randor. Denied the throne of Eternia in favor of his younger sibling, Keldor is damaged and dying, but determined to live to serve Hordak—and prepared to shed his half-brother's blood to transform himself into a new being, Skeletor. Frazer Irving's intense blue-green illustrations capture the bizarre moments of death and resurrection.

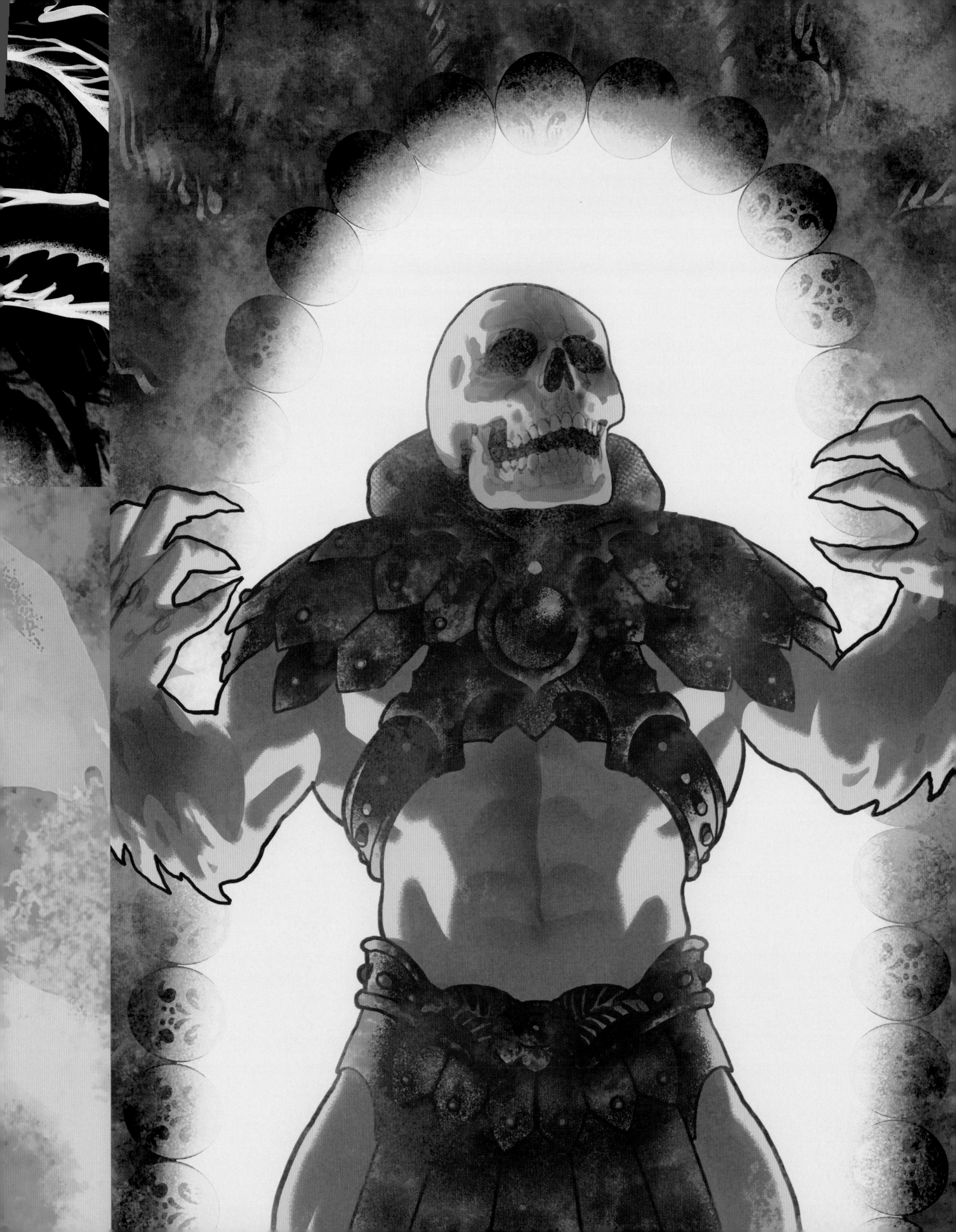

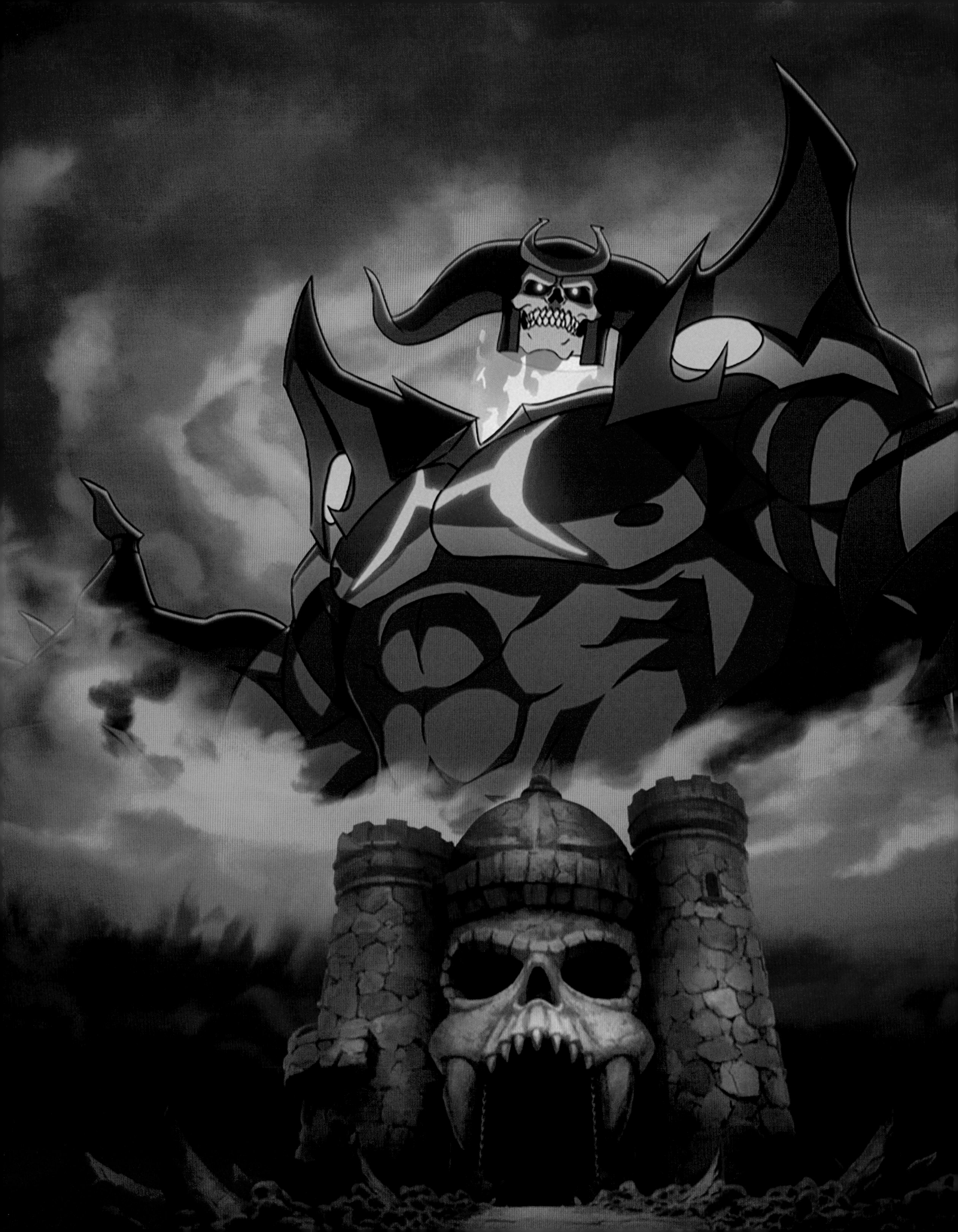

A NEW ERA

"We all have the power."

Rob David, Executive Producer, *Masters of the Universe: Revelation*, 2021

Skelegod arises *(left)* and He-Man on Battle Cat *(above)* from *Masters of the Universe: Revelation*

The Super7 Series

In 2016, toy makers Super7 took over the Masters of the Universe Classics toy line and created Ultimates, deluxe versions of the Classics figures. Super7 also returned Masters of the Universe to its roots with the first new, officially licensed vintage-style 5½-inch (14-cm) action figures. Packaged on blister cards that match the iconic red-and-blue "exploding rocks" of the originals, the figures in the line have the same articulation as the vintage line, with sculpts and detailing that more closely match the Filmation versions of the characters. The line launched in 2016 at San Diego Comic-Con with a brand-new Filmation-style animated short, "The Curse of the Three Terrors," which features newly invented characters, Terror Bat, Terror Jaguar, and Terror Wolf. The Super7 range also includes characters who originally did not appear in the vintage lines, such as Shadow Weaver and Eldor, a figure from the prototyped but unreleased "The Powers of Grayskull" spin-off line from the classic Masters of the Universe toy line. Some variant characters are inspired by incidents from the Filmation cartoon, including Robot He-Man, a translucent blue version of Teela called Frozen Teela, and Gold Statue He-Man. An inventive variant is Transforming He-Man, made of glow-in-the-dark white plastic, which depicts him in the middle of his transformation from Prince Adam to He-Man!

GOLD STATUE HE-MAN

HE-MAN

TEELA

Inspired by 1987 episode "The Ice Age Cometh"

FROZEN TEELA

MAN-AT-ARMS

ORKO

SHADOW ORKO

Glow-in-the-dark plastic

TRANSFORMING HE-MAN

SHE-RA

SKELETOR

POSSESSED SKELETOR

EVIL SEED

MER-MAN

BUZZ-OFF

Book of
Living Spells

ELDOR

"Hovers" on clear
plastic stand

SHADOW
WEAVER

TERROR BAT

STRATOS

Inspired by
1984 episode
"Disappearing Act"

TRAP JAW

BEAST MAN

ROBOT HE-MAN

Masters of the Universe Origins: Packaging Art

Launched at San Diego Comic-Con in 2019 with a deluxe two-pack of Prince Adam and He-Man, Masters of the Universe Origins begins a new era for He-Man. Origins reimagines the vintage 1980s range of 5½-inch (14-cm) action figures, remaining true to the originals but with an updated look and a higher level of articulation—16 working joints, including neck, shoulders, knees, hips, and more, giving greater options for play and display stances. The new figures include extra details for fans to spot, such as the knife tucked into He-Man's boot, a nod to early concept art of the character. The vintage-style packaging includes newly created artworks and reimagined minicomics.

RAGING BEAST
The powerful new cardback illustration for Beast Man features line art by
Axel Giménez and colors by Francisco Etchart.

HEROIC STEED

The box art for Battle Cat, released in 2020, features line artwork by Axel Giménez and colors by Francisco Etchart.

SKY BATTLE

The box art for the 2020 release of the Sky Sled, with Prince Adam figure, featured a battle above Castle Grayskull.

PRINCESS OF POWER

The Power-Con exclusive packaging for She-Ra unfolds to reveal a three-panel artwork, seen here, and contains an exclusive comic that reimagines She-Ra's origin story.

MOTU Origins Artwork

The Masters of the Universe Origins line features new action scenes on the packaging. Reminiscent of the vintage packaging art but freshly imagined, the new artworks are created by Nate Baertsch and colorist Francisco Etchart, though Val Staples provided art for the inaugural two-pack featuring He-Man and Prince Adam and Axel Giménez created art for the Castle Grayskull set.

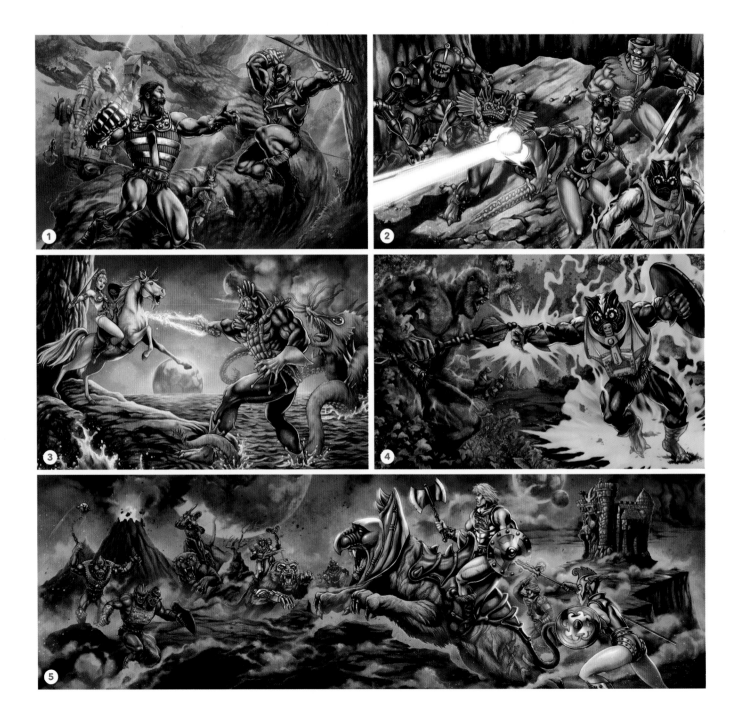

1 **Fisto** cardback (2021)
2 **Evil-Lyn** cardback, version 2 (2021)
3 **Mer-Man** cardback (2021)
4 **Stinkor** cardback (2021)
5 **Battle Damage He-Man and Battle Cat** cardback (2021)
6 **Hordak** cardback (2021)
7 **Tri-Klops** cardback (2020)
8 **Zodac** cardback (2021)
9 **Green Goddess** cardback (2021)
10 **Panthor** box art (detail) (2020)
11 **Keldor and Kronis** box art (detail) (2021)
12 **Ram Man** deluxe cardback (2021)

The incredible wraparound box artwork for Castle Grayskull, released in 2021 in the Masters of the Universe Origins toy line, features pencils by Axel Giménez and colors by Nate Baertsch. The artists were inspired by Rudy Obrero's art from the original Grayskull box and, particularly in the vibrant colors of the deep blue and pink sky, William George's poster art from the 1980s.

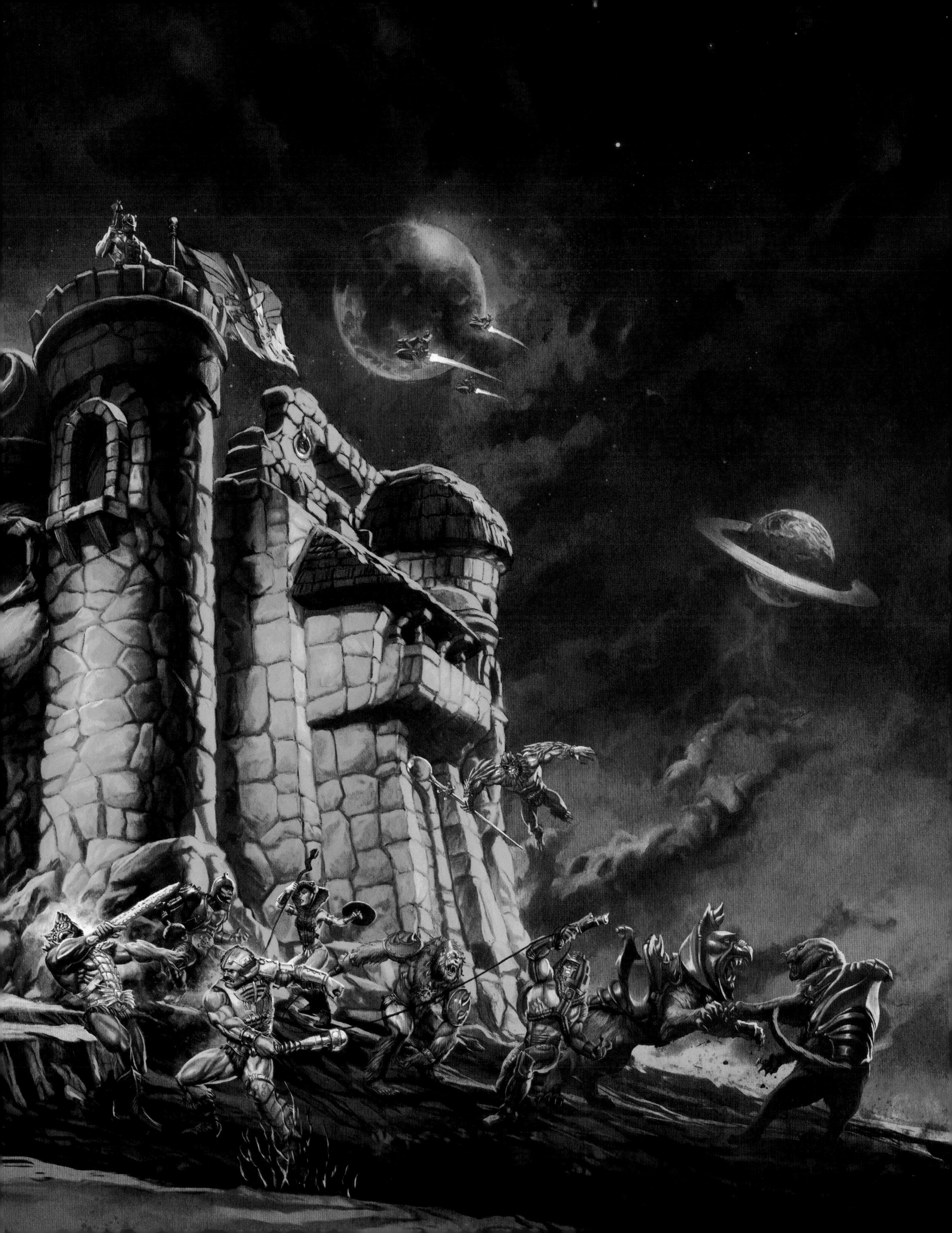

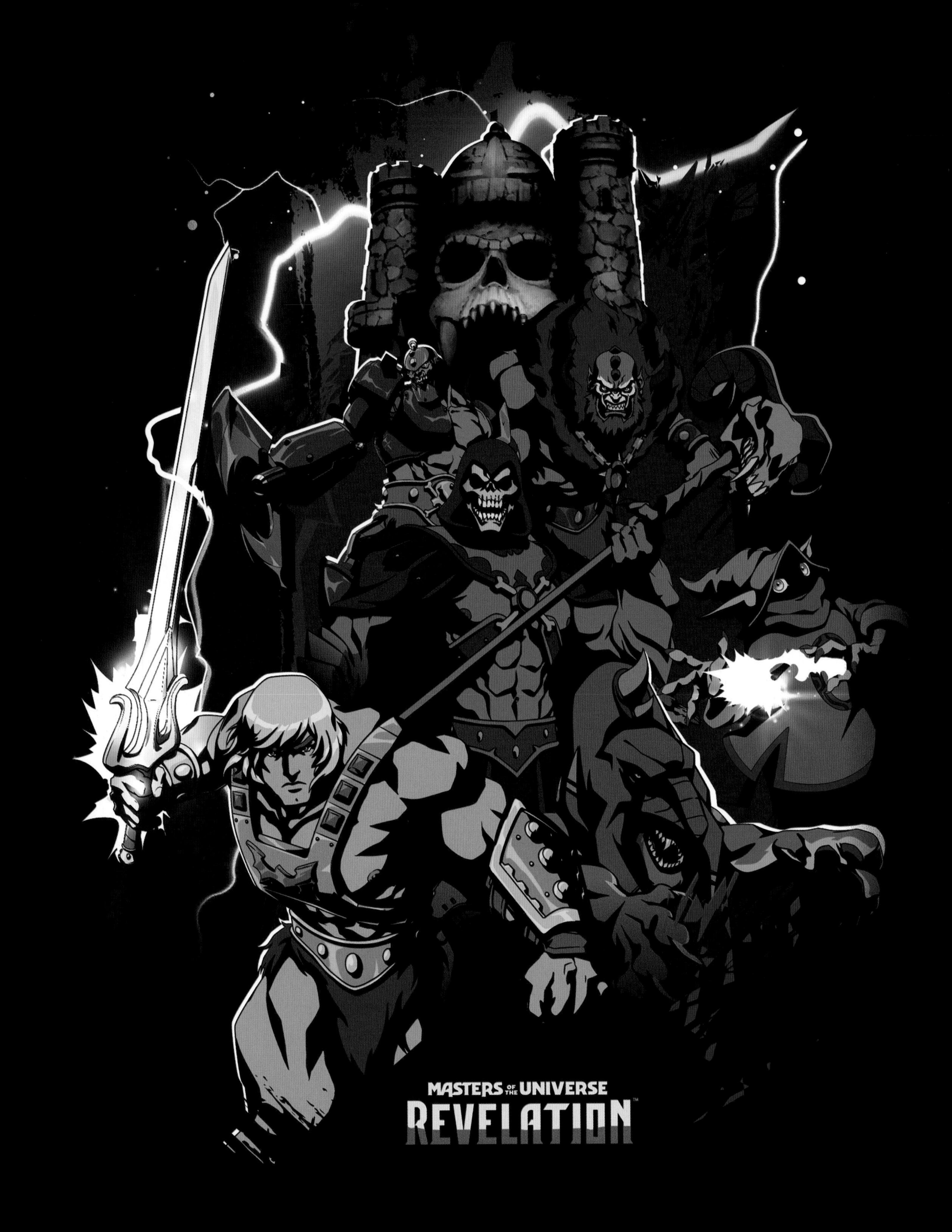
MASTERS OF THE UNIVERSE
REVELATION™

Masters of the Universe: Revelation

Returning to Eternia after more than 35 years, *Masters of the Universe: Revelation* picks up where the classic 1980s storyline left off.

At the MOTU fan convention Power-Con in August 2019, director Kevin Smith announced that he and Mattel Television were developing a new animated series for Netflix titled *Masters of the Universe: Revelation*. It would be a spiritual sequel to the canon of the 1980s, with surprises in store for every fan. Animated by Austin, Texas-based animation studio Powerhouse (*Castlevania*), the series features Prince Adam/He-Man, voiced by *Supergirl*'s Chris Wood, pitted, as ever, against his greatest foe Skeletor, voiced by *Star Wars*' Mark Hamill. Other voice cast includes *Buffy the Vampire Slayer*'s Sarah Michelle Gellar as Teela; *Game of Thrones*' Lena Headey as Evil-Lyn; *Clueless* star Alicia Silverstone as Queen Marlena; and the original voice of Skeletor, Alan Oppenheimer, now in the role of Moss Man. The show introduces characters from beyond the original Filmation series, including Teela's old friend Lieutenant Andra, who first appeared in comic books by Marvel Comics' imprint Star. Some of the show's characters only ever appeared as toys, such as Scare Glow and He-Ro. The creators have dug deep into the lore to bring back familiar and forgotten faces from every era, including from concept art created for the toy line back in the late 1970s and early 1980s.

FOR THE FANS

Mattel Television Executive Producer Rob David, who previously wrote and developed He-Man comics for DC Comics, described the show, which debuted in 2021, as "a love letter" for the fans who watched the original show as kids and are now adults. Ted Biaselli, director of original series at Netflix, adds that it delivers genuine stakes and high drama. Kevin Smith agrees: "In '*Revelation*,' we pick up right where the classic era left off to tell an epic tale of what may be the final battle between He-Man and Skeletor!"

"This is the Masters of the Universe story you always wanted to see as a kid!"

Kevin Smith, Executive Producer and Showrunner, *Masters of the Universe: Revelation*, 2019

Revelation: Heroic Warriors

With the royal court divided, magic under threat, and He-Man missing, Eternia is in need of new heroes: everyone plays their part as unexpected—and risky—alliances are formed, old wounds are reopened, and secrets are spilled. Eternia's past and present are explored and some familiar faces reappear, from former Heroic Warriors to some of the most ancient sages and heroes in Preternia.

ROYAL BUFFOON

Orko is up to his usual tricks—which still misfire—but he proves himself surprisingly useful in a crisis. However, in an Eternia where magic is under threat, his powers are also in danger.

MAN DOWN

He-Man finally gets to use the Sword of Power not just to transform, but to fight—with cataclysmic consequences.

MASTER WARRIOR

Man-At-Arms is still a devoted father to Teela, as well as the ungrateful recipient of Orko's magical efforts and a master warrior with superlative technical know-how.

WEAKENED WITCH

In an Eternia where magic itself is under threat, the Sorceress remains in Castle Grayskull, tending the dying embers of its power source.

CAPTAIN OF THE GUARD

Outfitted in her Captain of the Guard uniform, Teela is elevated to the position at court of Man-At-Arms, but it won't turn out to be for long.

HOVER-DISC RACING
In the forests of Preternia, Adam and Teela ride on hover discs with the Preternian sorceress of Grayskull, Kuduk, and a barbarian named Vikor.

TROUBLE-MAKER
Prince Adam's secret is out, and the shock waves reverberate through the royal court, turning families and friends against each other. Will the slothful prince be able to transform into He-Man ever again?

GOOD KITTY
Cringer knows his own fearful nature enough to recognize when others are afraid and need a pep talk. Is he getting wise in his old age?

CASTLE UNDER THREAT
Castle Grayskull faces the greatest threat of its long existence: the total extinction of its magical power source.

Revelation: Evil Warriors

With Skeletor seemingly out of the picture, his evil acolytes have turned against each other. Mer-Man returns to his underwater realm of Aquatica after Evil-Lyn refuses to join with him, while Beast Man retreats deep into the Eternian forest. Meanwhile, Evil-Lyn begins an uneasy alliance with Teela. Back in Snake Mountain, Tri-Klops and Trap Jaw preside over twisted ceremonies for turning ordinary Eternians into evil machine-hybrids—all in the name of their new faith in the "Motherboard." Where's Skeletor when evil needs him?

OVERLORD OF EVIL
Skeletor is determined to ransack Grayskull to steal all the power in the universe, and he is prepared to destroy the castle—and possibly himself—to do so!

METAL WORKER
Trap Jaw does what he has to do: chopping off arms from willing supplicants and attaching metal techno-tentacles, and worse!

DEMON OF DARKNESS
When Skeletor manages to activate the powers contained within the Power Sword, he transforms into a Skelegod!

ALL-SEEING PSYCHO
Tri-Klops is in the business of receiving acolytes who wish to become fused with machine parts, turning mediocre flesh into metallic monstrosities!

CITADEL OF FEAR
Snake Mountain is as creepy as ever, with demon faces peering out on all sides and swarming with robed, techno-enhanced cyborg guards.

DOUBLE-DEALER
Evil-Lyn is up to her old tricks, disguising herself as the benign sorceress Majestra but secretly harboring the desire to wrest ultimate power for herself—though she has to renew her alliance with Teela to further her plans.

FERAL FIGHTER
Beast Man no longer sees eye-to-eye with Tri-Klops and the other Evil Warriors, becoming a freelance fiend in Eternia's wild forests.

Revelation: New Alliances

When King Randor strips Man-At-Arms of his title and banishes him from the palace for hiding from him the secret of Prince Adam's true identity, Teela also quits in disgust that her own father kept the secret from her for so long. As Teela embarks on a new life as a mercenary and thief-for-hire with her old ally, Andra, she will find that the past—and her true nature—cannot be so easily left behind.

Tech-enhanced gauntlet

ROOTED IN GRAYSKULL
In Preternia, Adam receives wise words from Moss Man, who is both a giant treelike being who inhabits and protects the power core deep within Castle Grayskull and a human-sized figure—either way, this mystical creature smells of pine!

FAITHFUL FRIEND
Paired up with Teela in exile, Andra is a treasure-hunter for hire and an engineer, a useful skill in an Eternia where magic no longer works. She jokes that she is the "brains" to Teela's "brawn."

GRINNING EVIL

In the shadowy realms of Subternia, a glowing skull demon looms—Scare Glow, feeding on the power of fear and fright.

Regular battle outfit

DEADLY ENTRANCE

The Wolf Gates on Snake Mountain are covered with techno traps, deadly pressure sensors, and … general menace! Oh well, Teela and Andra must find a way to enter anyway.

HIRED HAND

Abandoning her role at the palace, Teela makes a living as a mercenary. Her magical staff can morph into different tools and weapons.

CLOUD OF STENCH

Living in garbage in a trash shack somewhere in Eternia, Stinkor guards what he calls his "merch" from "soap-stinkin fingers."

Masterverse

The vintage-but-stylized look of *Masters of the Universe: Revelation* carries through to Mattel's new toy line, Masters of the Universe: Masterverse. Teased at Power-Con Online in 2020 and launched in 2021, the highly detailed figures stand 7 inches (nearly 18 cm) tall with 30 points of articulation for maximum battle-stance action.

↑ He-Man and Battle Cat have an updated, stylized look. Battle Cat is 14 inches (35.5 cm) long with detachable armor and helmet that can be removed to reveal Cringer underneath.

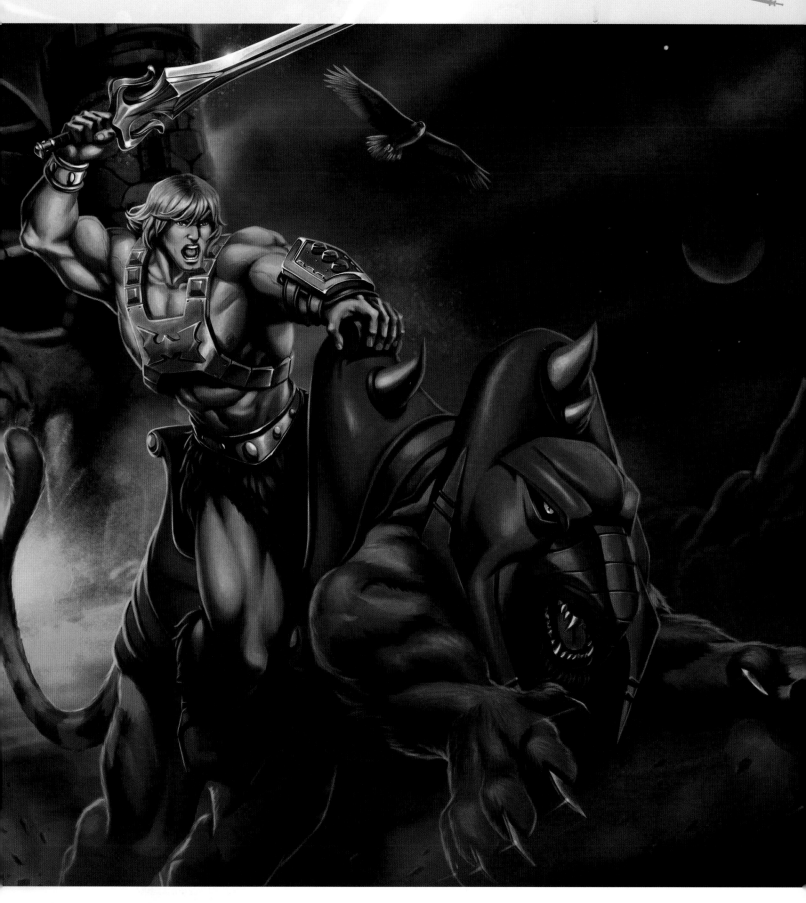

↑ He-Man and Battle Cat: Masterverse packaging art by Eamon O'Donoghue, with pencils by O'Donoghue and Eddie Nuñez.

↑ Skeletor has waited a long time for this! Finally, *finally* holding aloft He-Man's Power Sword for himself, the Lord of Destruction utters the words, "By the power of Grayskull! I have the power!" and behold: the Skelegod! Now he, Skeletor, is a Master of the Universe and revelation, truly, is upon us.

The first six action figures in the Masters of the Universe: Masterverse toy line, released in 2021, are 7-inch (nearly 18-cm) models of He-Man, Skeletor, Moss Man, and Evil-Lyn; a 9-inch (23-cm) model of Skelegod; and the 14-inch (35.5-cm) long Battle Cat. he figures come with accessories and, in some cases, interchangeable hands which allow them to hold accessories or pose without them.

↑ Skeletor's action figure comes with a pair of alternate hands, as well as his Havoc Staff and scepter.

No flocking on Moss Man but a cool new styling

↑ Evil-Lyn carries her wand and wears a redesigned battle outfit, with side bag.

Twisted-vine arm attachment

↑ Moss Man is the only "mythical Preternian plant creature" Adam knows—and one of the most powerful beings in Eternia.

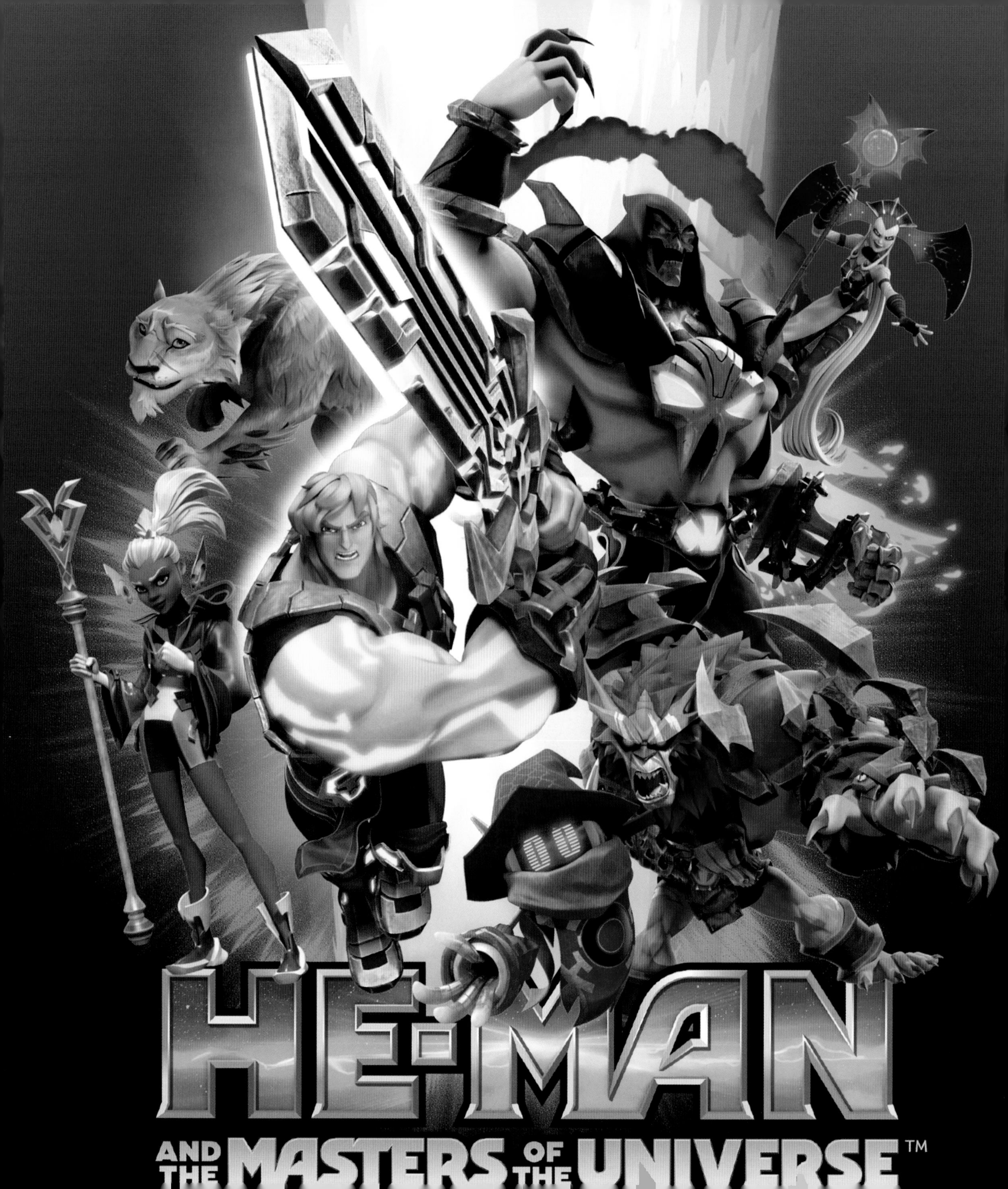
HE-MAN
AND THE MASTERS OF THE UNIVERSE ™

A New Beginning

The 2021 CGI show *He-Man and the Masters of the Universe* is a fresh take on the classic tale.

Produced by Mattel Television for Netflix, *He-Man and the Masters of the Universe* comes hot on the heels of Dreamworks' *She-Ra and the Princesses of Power*, which ran for five seasons between 2018 and 2020. The new show is animated by House of Cool (*Ferdinand*) and CGCG (*Star Wars: Resistance*). Executive producer and showrunner Rob David developed the series for television. Jeff Matsuda serves as co-executive producer, Susan Corbin as producer, Melanie Shannon as creative executive, and Bryan Q. Miller as story editor. This series explores the themes of self-discovery and more specifically what it means to be a Master of the Universe.

A FAMILY OF HEROES

In the new series, teenage Adam, his best friend Krass, and pet tiger Cringer live in an Eternian jungle village—an echo of the early minicomics mythos. Teela is a thief who has stolen a sword from the Royal Palace on behalf of two villains named Evelyn and Kronis. The sword interacts with Adam's gold wrist cuff and before he knows it, he's intoning the words, "By the power of Grayskull …" With the addition of airship pilot Duncan, the new "family" follows the voices in Teela's head and heads for Castle Grayskull. "So if we find the castle," says Adam, "we can learn about … well, everything." Meanwhile, a mysterious figure reappears: Keldor …

"Everyone longs to discover the one thing they were born to do."

Rob David, Executive Producer and Showrunner, *He-Man and the Masters of the Universe, 2021*

↓ Would-be heroes Duncan, Krass, Adam, Cringer, and Teela are about to discover their true powers and potential.

The Power of Grayskull

Evelyn is desperate to get her hands on the sword that Teela has stolen from the Royal Palace; she knows it contains the Power of Grayskull. In the confrontation, Teela hands it to Adam when, suddenly, the cuff on his wrist and the sword connect—the sword begins glowing with gold energy as stormy air swirls around him! He haltingly reads the words circling the sword: "By the Power of Grayskull ... I have the power?" The golden energy from the sword becomes a vortex of power and lightning crackles off Adam as his veins pop and his muscles bulge. As the others watch, teenaged Adam has been transformed. "He's ... a man," Krass marvels. "The Power of Grayskull," Teela murmurs in awe.

↑ The CGI *He-Man and the Masters of the Universe* series reimagines Adam's first transformation into He-Man, as he begins to discovers for the first time his true origins.

↑ Connecting the sword to his gold cuff connects Adam to his past as heir to the throne of Eternia—something that, at the start of the series, he had no idea about.

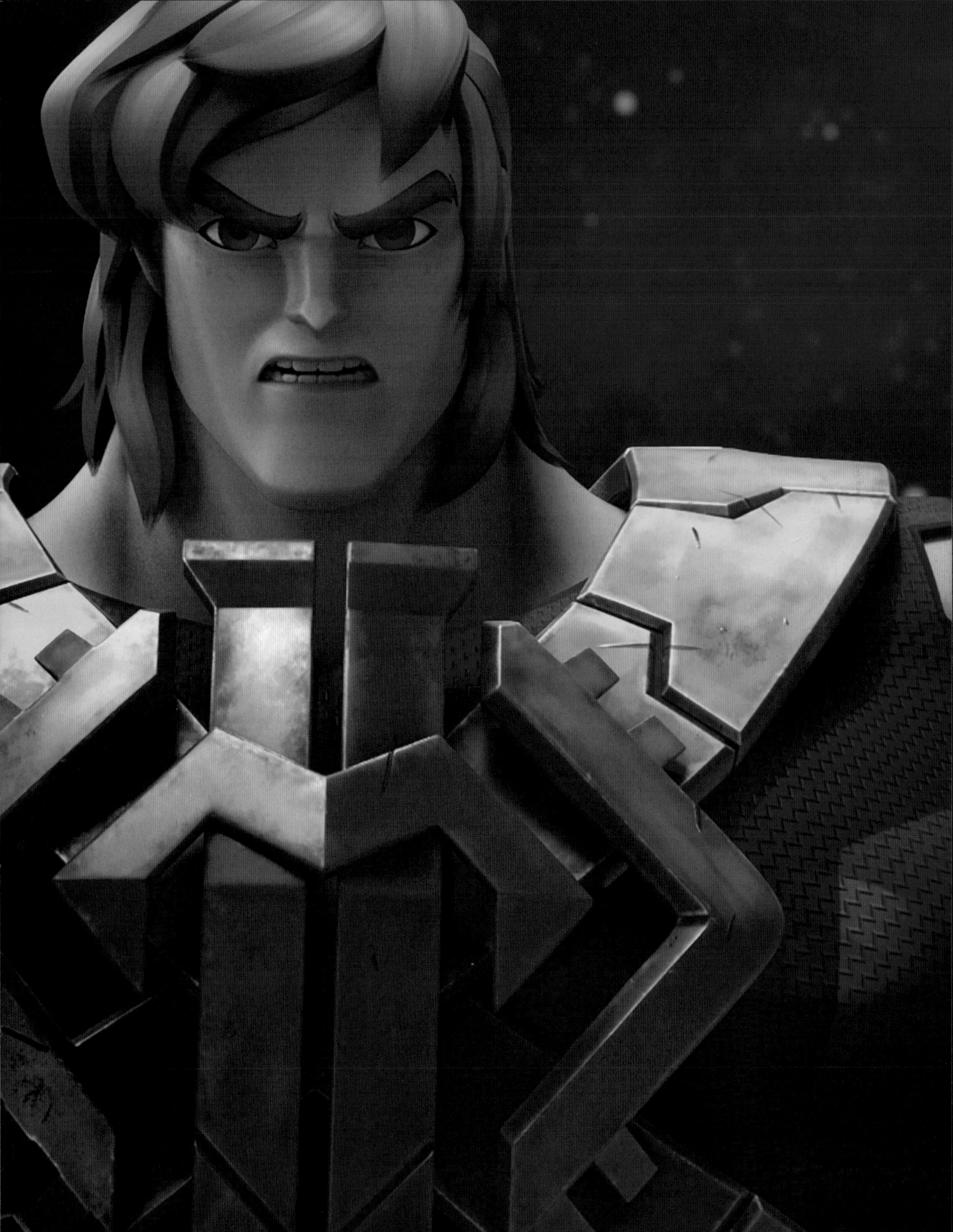

We Have the Power!

Captured by Keldor, Evil-Lyn, and Kronis in Castle Grayskull, Adam decides that he wants to share the power with his friends. They aren't sure it will work, but Teela hears the voice in her head which assures her of success. Feeding off the energy within the castle itself, He-Man raises his sword and yells, "By the Power of Grayskull!" Grayskull's power crackles onto each friend's special item: Teela's staff, Duncan's multitool, Krass's helmet, and Cringer's claws. They each yell "I have the Power!" as they transform. Finally, He-Man declares, "WE have the power!"

CRINGER,
BATTLE CAT

DUNCAN,
MAN-AT-ARMS

KRASS,
RAM MA'AM

> "To know oneself is to truly become ...
> a Master of the Universe."
>
> The Spirit of Grayskull

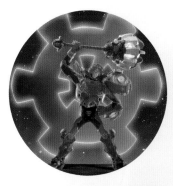

WINGED SORCERESS
Teela becomes a winged sorceress ... but does more falling than flying at first. "Flap your wings," Duncan advises her.

WRECKING BALL
Krass's power helm generates energy that enables her to ping around like a "literal ram ball." She quickly dubs herself "Ram Ma'am."

MASTER OF WEAPONS
With his powerful new mace weapon, Duncan exclaims, "I think I just got promoted to Man-at-Arms for Castle Grayskull!"

CLAWS OUT!
"Battle Cat is on the way," says Cringer after his transformation, naming himself before anyone else does.

ADAM,
HE-MAN

TEELA,
THE SORCERESS

HERO TEAM
The new hero team is equipped, powered-up, and ready for action.

The Rise of Skeletor

Keldor returns after "convalescing in stasis for ten years"—and immediately he's furious because no one came to rescue him. All of Eternos believed he died the night of the coup ... when he kidnapped the King's son—his own nephew. Now he is on his way back to Castle Grayskull to finish what he started. On the night of the coup, he tried to seize Grayskull's power, but the castle's guardian—the Sorceress—gave him a choice: the sword or the scepter. Viewing the sword as the tool of a soldier—a servant to power—he chose the scepter: "the totem of a true ruler."

However, his choice inflicted him with the blight of Havoc. The Sorceress tells Keldor that "The Power of Grayskull can only be commanded by a true champion," meaning Adam, setting uncle against nephew. Now he has returned to unleash his Havoc powers. A new era has begun!

↑ Keldor reappears, ready to assume command of those around him, starting with Evil-Lyn, who can only pretend that she's pleased to see him again.

↗ Furious that the Sword of Power changes Adam into He-Man, Keldor takes up arms against his own young nephew. "A champion isn't some child playing at being a man!" he snarls.

→ Giving into Havoc power, Keldor begins to transform, laughing maniacally.

> # "The age of Grayskull has passed ... welcome to the age of ... Skeletor!"
>
> Skeletor,
> "The Champions of Grayskull," 2021

← Keldor, now as Skeletor, uses his hideous new Havoc powers to form an abandoned ruin into the terrifying shape of ... Snake Mountain!

↓ Skeletor drops his plans to wield Grayskull's light. "I will usher in an era of brimstone and blight," he declares, "... with the purity of ... Havoc!"

Dark Masters

The heroes converge on Snake Mountain where, unnervingly, Skeletor simply opens his door and welcomes them in. In a sacrificial chamber, the heroes see Keldor for the first time in his horrifying new form as Skeletor. Suddenly his minions appear: Evelyn; Kronis; and his new recruit, the vicious Rqazz. "We won't let you use your weapon against Eternos," says He-Man. Skeletor and Evelyn laugh maniacally. "We ARE the weapons," Evelyn sneers as each minion transforms into the evil nemeses of the Heroic Warriors. Skeletor commands: "Rise, my Dark Masters … and wreak Havoc!"

MASTER OF WITCHCRAFT
Evelyn becomes Evil-Lyn, powerful sorceress and Skeletor's right hand. She is the most talented of the Dark Masters, carrying her Orb of Witchcraft and wearing her Wings of Horokoth.

EVIL-LYN

DARK TRANSFORMATION
Skeletor lifts his staff and shouts, "Through the Purity of Havoc …" Green havoc swirls as he slams the staff into the ground, adding, "They have MY power!" Havoc erupts from Skeletor's staff, chaining each of his minions to him as they painfully transform.

MASTER OF WEAPONRY

Kronis transforms into Trap Jaw, creator of tools and vehicles of destruction for Skeletor and his fellow Dark Masters.

TRAP JAW

MASTER OF BEASTS

Rqazz transforms into the overlord of all snarling beasts and monsters, Beast Man. He has heightened senses and a ferocious temper, causing wild mayhem wherever he goes.

BEAST MAN

Index of Characters

Sources

James Eatock, *He-Man and the Masters of the Universe: A Complete Guide to the Classic Animated Adventures* (Dark Horse, 2016)
Randall Lobb, Robert McCallum, *Power of Grayskull: The Definitive History of He-Man and the Masters of the Universe* (Definitive Film/Pyre Productions, 2017)
Adam McCombs, "Bob Nall: Heroic Master of Toy Packaging," Battle Ram: A He-Man Blog, July 3, 2019
Adam McCombs, "Ted Mayer: Virtuoso of Vehicle Design," Battle Ram: A He-Man Blog, December 14, 2015
Maurice Mitchell, "McQuarrie Almost Brought The Power of Greyskull To 'Masters of the Universe,'" filmsketchr.blogspot.com, April 19, 2012
Tim Seeley, Steven Grant, Phil White, Robert Kirkman, Michael Halperin, Scott Neitlich,

He-Man and the Masters of the Universe: Minicomic Collection (Dark Horse, 2015)
Tim Seeley, Steve Seeley, *The Art of He-Man and the Masters of the Universe* (Dark Horse, 2015)
James Shull, Chris Weber, Karen Willson, *He-Man and the Masters of the Universe: The Newspaper Comic Strips* (Dark Horse, 2017)
Val Staples, "Pixel" Dan Eardley, *The Toys of He-Man and the Masters of the Universe* (Dark Horse, 2021)
Val Staples, Josh de Lioncourt, James Eatock, Danielle Gelehrter, *He-Man and the Masters of the Universe: A Character Guide and World Compendium* (Dark Horse, 2017)
Tallstar, "Princess of Power Secrets Revealed Part 1," He-Man.Org, November 5, 2012
Tom Stern, *The Toys that Made Us: He-Man* (Netflix, 2017)

Picture Credits

Project Editor Rosie Peet
Senior Designer Anna Formanek
Senior Production Editor Marc Staples
Senior Production Controller Louise Minihane
Managing Editor Paula Regan
Design Manager Jo Connor
Publishing Director Mark Searle

Written by Simon Beecroft
Designed by Lisa Lanzarini

First American Edition, 2021
Published in the United States by DK Publishing
1450 Broadway, Suite 801, New York, NY 10018

Page design copyright © 2021 Dorling Kindersley Limited
DK, a Division of Penguin Random House LLC
21 22 23 24 25 10 9 8 7 6 5 4 3 2 1
001–321712– Dec/2021

© 1982-2021 Mattel Inc.

A catalog record for this book
is available from the Library of Congress.
ISBN 978-0-7440-2722-8

DK books are available at special discounts when purchased in bulk
for sales promotions, premiums, fund-raising, or educational use.
For details, contact: DK Publishing Special Markets,
1450 Broadway, Suite 801, New York, NY 10018
SpecialSales@dk.com

Printed and bound in China

ACKNOWLEDGMENTS
DK would like to thank Adam McCombs from Battle Ram Blog,
the fans at He-Man.Org, and Val Staples for fact checking;
Joe Teague and Brian Obman for additional photography;
Val Staples for photo restoration; Rowenna Otazu, Rob David,
and Ryan Ferguson at Mattel; Julia March for indexing;
Kayla Dugger for proofreading; Martin Copeland, Sumedha
Chopra, Vagisha Pushp, and Deepak Negi for picture research.

For the curious
www.dk.com

Mattel.com

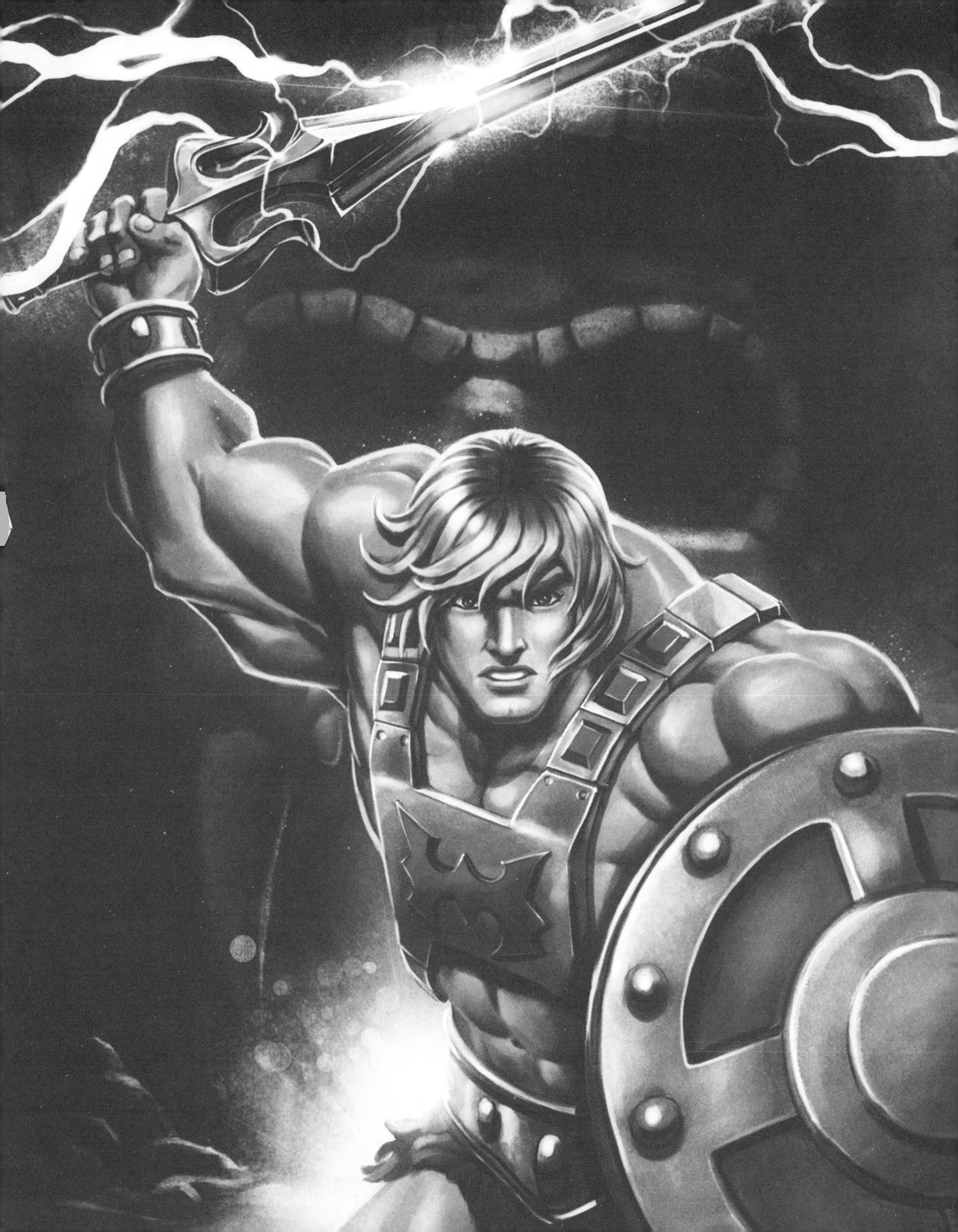